PLAN
FOR
PROFITABILITY!

HOW TO WRITE
A STRATEGIC
BUSINESS PLAN

PLAN
FOR
PROFITABILITY!

HOW TO WRITE
A STRATEGIC
BUSINESS PLAN

by
Lee E. Hargrave, Jr.

The Hargrave Consultancy
http://www.hargrave.com
hargrave@hargrave.com

PLAN
FOR
PROFITABILITY!

HOW TO WRITE
A STRATEGIC
BUSINESS PLAN

All rights reserved
Copyright ©1999 Lee E. Hargrave Jr.

Reproduction in any manner, in whole or in part,
in English or in other languages, or otherwise
without written permission of publisher is prohibited.

For information contact: Four Seasons Publishers
P.O.Box 51, Titusville, FL 32781

PRINTING HISTORY
First Printing 1999

ISBN 1-891929-19-4

PRINTED IN THE UNITED STATES OF AMERICA
1 2 3 4 5 6 7 8 9 10

In memory of Robbie and Lee Hargrave

As the twig is bent, the tree's inclined.
Alexander Pope, 1731

TABLE OF CONTENTS

ABOUT THE AUTHOR   i

CHAPTER 1: SOME FUNDAMENTALS   1
    Strategic Business Planning   3
    The Evolution of This Book   5
    Strategic Business Units   8
    The Responsibility for Strategic Planning   11
    Introducing International Microwidgets   15
    Summary   19

**CHAPTER II: THE STRUCTURE OF
A STRATEGIC PLAN**   20
    The Annual Planning Cycle   22
    The Planning Horizon   25
    The Flow of a Strategic Plan   27
    The Mission   31
    Mission Statements   32
    The Mission of International Microwidgets   36
    Summary   39

CHAPTER III: THE MARKET   41
    The Served Market   44
    Market Segmentation   47
    Sources of Market Data   52
    Quantifying the Market   53
    Market Measurements   56
    Chronological Market Data   57
    Market Cycles   62
    Statistical Projection Techniques   66
    The Market of International Microwidgets   72
    Summary   74

CHAPTER IV: COMPETITION   76
    Market Share   78
    Chronological Market Share Data   82
    Sources of Competitive Data   83
    Competitors' Strengths and Weaknesses   87
    Listing Strengths and Weaknesses   89
    Competitors' Strategies   91
    The Strategy Summary   92
    The Competitors of International Microwidgets   94
    Summary   102

**CHAPTER V: CONSOLIDATING
       THE ENVIRONMENT**   106
    SBU Strengths and Weaknesses   108
    Determining Opportunities and Threats   112
    Listing Opportunities and Threats   115
    The Learning Curve   116
    The Original Portfolio Matrix   120
    The Nine-Block Matrix   123
    The Environment of International Microwidgets   127
    Summary   130

**CHAPTER VI: OBJECTIVES, STRATEGIES,
       PROGRAMS AND GOALS**   133
    Definitions   134
    The Principle of Linkages   138
    Objectives   142
    Strategies   148
    Programs   150
    Goals   152
    International Microwidgets   154
    Summary   159

CHAPTER VII: RESOURCES 161
    People 162
    Facilities 164
    Equipment 169
    Transition to the Financial Statements 169
    Resource Projections 171
    International Microwidgets 178
    Summary 180

CHAPTER VIII: FINANCIAL PROJECTIONS 183
    Financial Statements 186
    Revenue Projections 188
    The Operating Statement 190
    The Balance Sheet 201
    The Funds Flow Statement 208
    International Microwidgets 208
    Summary 213

CHAPTER IX: EVALUATING THE PLAN 215
    Gross Margin 217
    Return Measurements 217
    The Use of Leverage 223
    Debt versus Equity 227
    Operating Efficiency Measurements 230
    Trend Analysis 234
    Evaluation of the International
    Microwidgets Plan 238
    Summary 242

CHAPTER X:BEYOND STRATEGIC PLANNING 244
    The Operational Plan   245
    The Three S's   250
    Organizational Structures   252
    Line andStaffFunctions   257
    A Representative Company Organization   258
    The Concept of Corporate Developement   261
    Summary   262

CHAPTER XI: CORPORATE DEVELOPMENT   264
    Entering and Exiting Businesses   264
    Secondary Valuation Techniques   268
    The Concept of Net Present Value   270
    Mergers versus Acquisitions   276
    Goodwill   278
    Dilution   280
    The Acquisition of General Widgets   285
    Summary   289

CHAPTER XII: THE STRATEGIC PLAN OF
    INTERNATIONAL MICROWIDGETS   291

ABOUT THE AUTHOR

Lee Hargrave began his business career as an electronics engineer at the National Security Agency, Sanders Associates, and his own engineering company. From engineering, his career progressed through a succession of increasing responsibilities in project management, international operations, strategic business planning, and general management.

After 14 years with General Electric, he spent five years as Vice President of Corporate Planning and Development for Storage Technology Corporation, two years as Chief Operating Officer of Computer Automation, Inc., and five years as President and CEO of CASI-RUSCO, Inc., a manufacturer of computer-based access control systems.

Since 1991, Mr. Hargrave has been the principal of The Hargrave Consultancy and has specialized in assisting companies to anticipate change through strategic business planning and to achieve it through rigorous attention to operating plans.

He holds a BA in Mathematics and a BS in Electrical Engineering from the University of Pennsylvania, an MS in Electrical Engineering from the University of Maryland, and an MBA from Drexel University. He is a member of five scholastic honor societies, the author of two books and several articles, and a member of Mensa.

As an avocation to his business career, Mr. Hargrave has taught an eclectic range of courses at four colleges and universities: Electrical Engineering at the University of Maryland, Organization Theory at Catholic University, Strategic

Lee E. Hargrave, Jr.

Business Planning at the University of Colorado, and Business and Computer Science at Indian River Community College.

A resident of Florida since 1987, he is married with grown children. His active interests include skiing, tennis, squash, golf and physical fitness. Reflective interests include music, bridge and practicing French and German.

CHAPTER I

SOME FUNDAMENTALS

I have always thought that one man of tolerable abilities may work great changes, and accomplish great affairs among mankind, if he first forms a good plan, and, cutting off all amusements or other employments that would divert his attention, make the execution of that same plan his sole study and business.

Benjamin Franklin,
written 1771-90, published 1868

It does not matter how small you are if you have faith and plan of action.

Fidel Castro, 1959

A survey by Arthur Andersen of 966 small businesses revealed that only 28% of them had written strategic business plans. However, those companies with written plans had:

- 40% more export business,

- 63% higher revenue growth, and

- 100% higher profits.

Why? A strategic business plan helps businesses to anticipate change and to communicate the company's action plan to all employees. The payoff of competent and thoughtful strategic planning is dramatic, as witnessed by the above statistics.

To be sure, there are many books on strategic planning. Most of them, however, are written by academicians, not business people. They abound with theory and advanced concepts, but generally lack the practical experience and hands-on guidance to enable the reader to create an effective strategic plan.

Let me tell you something about myself. I am a former Chief Executive Officer who now specializes in assisting businesses to plan for and achieve profitable change. In my 35-year career, I have written over 100 strategic plans, ranging from companies with over $1 billion in revenues to startup businesses with no revenues whatsoever.

This book is targeted for the individual who needs guidance in writing a strategic plan. A representative reader might include a small business owner without any exposure to strategic planning, an entrepreneur seeking venture capital to start up a new business, a manager in a corporate bureaucracy, an aspiring strategic planner and many others.

The book guides you through the interrelated elements of a typical plan: mission, market, competition, self-evaluation, opportunities and threats, objectives, strategies, programs, goals, resources and financials, including diverse examples from actual strategic plans. It contains all of the tools for even a novice to create a credible strategic plan.

STRATEGIC BUSINESS PLANNING

So, I proceed on the premise that you need to prepare a strategic business plan. Let me assure you that you have come to the right source for guidance. I have lost track of exactly how many strategic plans I have written over my business career, but, as I just mentioned, I estimate them to number more than 100.

Not only have there been a lot of them, but they have also varied in size and complexity. There have been plans for big companies with over $1 billion in annual revenues and for startup companies without any revenues at all. Some of the smaller companies consisted of a single strategic business unit, while many of the larger ones had multiple strategic business units.

In addition to writing strategic plans myself, I have also advised others who were developing plans. Here are profiles of some (but by no means all) of the strategic planning situations that I have encountered:

- A start-up company searching for venture capital that needed a strategic plan to present to potential investors;

- A company that had grown to Fortune 500 status in an opportunistic market niche with no formal strategic planning whatsoever;

- A company with a comprehensive strategic planning system for its domestic businesses, but without an integrated view of its business strategies in countries outside of the United States;

● A company that was expanding its business from a single line of products to multiple product lines;

● A company without any prior strategic planning (and substantial resistance in the ranks to change).

Perhaps you can identify with one or more of the foregoing scenarios. Regardless, if you need to write a strategic plan, the approach outlined in this book has been honed over many years, companies and scenarios. It should apply to your situation.

Before we start, however, we need to lay a foundation. What is strategic planning? (In this book, I will use the terms strategic plan and strategic business plan interchangeably without any intended difference in meaning.) In all of my reading on the subject, I have never encountered a universal definition. In fact, strategic plans exist under a variety of aliases such as long-range plans, forward plans, business plans, five-year plans and sundry more.

One of my parent companies even referred to its strategic plans as *hardcore plans*. Believe me, there was nothing X-rated about their plans, although some of them could be described as fiction. The term *hardcore* was intended to convey that the plan was inviolate; once approved by the Chairman, the business manager could not change it. This is a fallacious approach to planning because business environments change, necessitating that plans change too. More will be said about this in Chapter IX.

In my view, strategic planning is the process of determining the most appropriate direction for the evolution of a company's business and identifying those steps that must be taken in the near term to initiate (or continue) the evolution. In other words, it is the process of determining how the company should expect to be positioned at some time in the future and what steps should be taken in the near term to move toward that positioning. One of the first steps in developing a strategic plan is to identify the strategic business units (SBU's) that comprise the company.

THE EVOLUTION OF THIS BOOK

I was first introduced to strategic business planning in 1970 when I was with General Electric. In a pioneering move, GE, assisted by the management consulting firm, McKinsey and Company, instituted strategic business planning on a company-wide basis. It is important to understand that, at that time, strategic business planning was an initiative concept and its introduction across a company as large as GE was an ambitious undertaking. Nonetheless, corporate direction mandated that every business unit within the company was required to develop, from scratch, a strategic business plan within a time frame of less than a year.

The undertaking was further complicated by the fact that few people in the company had ever heard of strategic business planning and that even less knew anything about the subject. To address this deficiency, the company established a strategic business planning curriculum at its famed management institute in Crotonville, New York, and I was asked to attend a week-long course, after which I returned to my parent operation to assist in developing their plan. In short, I was present at the creation of strategic business planning and have been practicing the craft ever since.

Two years later, I was put in total charge of the annual plan for my strategic business unit. (I will define that term in a few pages; please bear with me.) Ours was a large business with almost $1 billion in revenues and plants in ten states. After that I transferred to GE's headquarters for Europe and the Middle East in Brussels, where I integrated the planning for 43 strategic business units.

In 1979, I joined Storage Technology Corporation as Vice President of Corporate Development, where I established the strategic planning process and directed it for several years. It was while I was there that Dean William Baughn of the College of Business Administration of the University of Colorado asked me to teach a course on strategic planning to senior-year business students.

My search for an appropriate text for the course left me with two distinct impressions. First, I could not find a single text that covered all of the topics that were essential to a thorough treatment of the subject. Second, most of the relevant texts were authored by academicians, as opposed to business people, and their material often left me with impressions of detachment and theory, rather than experience and practicality.

As a result, I developed my own set of lecture notes and materials, drawing from my diverse experience in both domestic and international business, coupled with an innate liking for the learning and teaching environment. The process of evolution and refinement ultimately resulted in the material that you are about to read.

I advanced into general management after Storage Technology and, while I continued to practice my planning craft, this material lay fallow in the late 1980's and early 1990's as the pressures of managing companies left little time for anything else. When I founded my own consulting business, however, I found that I was able to free up some time to complete the book.

In short, this book took over 15 years to complete. When one considers that it represents a lifetime of business observations, the elapsed time seems more reasonable.

Initially, as the material began to evolve, I envisioned it as a textbook in the college teaching environment. In time, however, I realized that what I was developing could better serve as a practical handbook for any businessperson who needs to prepare a strategic business plan.

There are, I believe, some original concepts presented in this material, though it is sometimes difficult as time passes to discern originality from mere improvements on the ideas of others. At the very least, I can justifiably claim that my interpretation of the subject is better organized than most other books I have read.

Most of the examples in this text are also drawn from my own background in business. I have made no attempt whatsoever to change any of the dates of the plans that serve as examples. Like football or basketball, the rules of the game of business may change gradually over time, but the objectives and the lessons learned remain constant. So, if the example serves its purpose, it should be immaterial whether it is vintage 1950 or 1990.

As I put this book together, I came to realize that there were pros and cons to using plans that I had actually developed as examples in the book. On the positive side, of course, is the fact that they are real plans and not theoretical examples. One seldom gets to see real strategic business plans since they are usually regarded as company proprietary information and protected accordingly. Sufficient time has elapsed, however, since the time frame of the examples in this book that no vestige of proprietary content could conceivably remain.

The downside to using actual examples is that many of the plans did not turn as they were intended. The harsh reality is that they seldom do, a fact that is overlooked in most business school curricula. I always considered a plan to be a success if most of the objectives, particularly the important ones, were achieved. Where the plans that you will encounter as you read on were less than successful, I will own up to the fact and attempt to explain the circumstances that mitigated success.

STRATEGIC BUSINESS UNITS

In the late 1960's, the concept of the strategic business unit began to emerge as the result of an innovative collaboration between General Electric and McKinsey and Company. This concept proposed that, regardless of the organizational structure of a company, it could be divided into a specific number of logical businesses (SBU's), each of which could be viewed as a free-standing business in itself. Keeping in place its existing organizational structure, in 1970 General Electric overlaid a set of 43 SBU's on the structure, with the SBU's ranging in size from less than $100 million in annual revenues to over $1 billion.

It should be emphasized that the SBU concept does not necessarily promote that the organizational structure of a company be conformed such that each SBU is segregated and self-sufficient within the structure. Rather, the SBU is the fundamental entity for which a complete strategic business plan can be developed. The proposition is that any company can be divided into a discrete number of SBU's such that the sum of the businesses of the SBU's equals the totality of the business of the company without overlaps or gaps between SBU's.

There are as many definitions of an SBU as there are authors on the subject. The management consulting firm of Arthur D. Little (ADL) has a definition that appeals to me because of its conciseness. ADL postulates that an SBU is "a business area with an external marketplace for its goods and services for which one can determine objectives and execute strategies independent of other business areas."[1]

Although a high degree of judgment is involved in defining the SBU's that comprise a given company, consensus can usually be reached among the management of a company regarding the least common set of SBU's that characterize the company. Most small companies are single SBU's in themselves, and even very large companies with revenues in the billion-dollar range may also be single SBU's.

---

[1] Arthur D. Little, Inc., A Management System for the 1980's, San Francisco, 1979

9

Conceptually, an SBU is characterized by:

- A relatively homogeneous set of products or services. Small household appliances such as toasters, irons and coffee makers would probably be combined into the same SBU. On the other hand, it would be inappropriate to include large appliances such as refrigerators, freezers, washers and dryers (which are collectively referred to in the trade as white goods) in the same SBU because of their disparities (vis-à-vis small appliances) in such considerations as the physical size of the product, price, magnitude of the buying decision and route to market.

- A definable and quantifiable market that the business serves, and an identifiable set of competitors against which the business competes for its share of the market. The concepts of served market and market share are intrinsic to the process of strategic business planning and are discussed in detail in Chapters III and IV.

- The ability to create free-standing financial statements, both historical and projected, for the business, especially an operating statement and a balance sheet. This is not meant to imply that an SBU need necessarily be a profit-and-loss center in the company, i.e., an entity for which operating statements, balance sheets and funds flow statements are routinely prepared as mechanisms for measuring operating performance. More often than not, however, SBU's are also profit-and-loss centers.

Plan For Profitability!

In summary, you must develop a strategic plan for each SBU within the company. This is because an SBU serves a unique market with a unique set of competitors from other SBU's. If yours is a small company, it is likely that you are a single SBU; in other words, you serve a single, definable market with a definable set of competitors.

If your company is larger, it is possible that you will identify two or more SBU's that comprise your business. You will need to develop a strategic business plan for each SBU, and your company's strategic plan will be the composite of the plans of the individual SBU's.

THE RESPONSIBILITY FOR STRATEGIC PLANNING

Make no mistake about it. The responsibility for strategic business planning rests squarely on the shoulders of the person who is running the business. Whether he or she is called the owner, boss, manager, president, managing director, general manager, chief executive officer, chief operating officer, chairman, manager-boss or any other title, the strategic plan must represent the views of the person in charge.

Manager-boss? I one held this exalted title for a day. In the late 1960's, I led a German-American consortium in the competitive pursuit of a $50 million spacecraft program (which we won, incidentally). One of our team members was the German electronics company, AEG-Telefunken, which was located in Ulm, Germany. They anticipated my first visit to their plant with admirable efficiency, even to the extent of preregistering me with the receptionist. As I signed the visitor's log, I noted that I

11

was preregistered as:

Name:	Herr Hargrave
Company:	General Electric
Title:	Manager-Boss.

From here on in this guidebook, I will refer to the person in charge of the company for which you are writing a strategic plan as the Chief Executive Officer, or CEO for short. Also, I will use the pronoun he to refer to either he or she and avoid the resulting awkward grammatical constructions.

It is the CEO who owns the plan. True, he may delegate the responsibility for its preparation to others. As I mentioned, I have sat in the chairs of these "others" many times with titles such as Manager of Strategic Planning and Vice President of Corporate Development. Although the CEO may delegate the responsibility for developing the strategic plan to others, he cannot shirk ownership of the resulting product. This implies that the CEO must review the planning as it evolves and sign off on the plan when it is finished.

What type of person does it take to be an effective strategic planner? Many of the hallmarks of an effective planner are identically those of an effective CEO. Not surprisingly, not everyone is suited to the task. In fact, in my experience, few individuals measure up to its demanding requisites.

Among the hallmarks of an effective strategic planner are:

Plan For Profitability!

- A broad and well-rounded educational background. The ability to read financial statements is mandatory.

- A history of working experience in many of the functions that comprise a modern business enterprise, especially engineering, manufacturing, marketing, finance and general management.

- The ability to reason in both the abstract and the concrete. An aptitude for inductive (right-brain) reasoning is particularly relevant, in that the strategic planner frequently must synthesize a panoramic view from sundry, seemingly isolated observations. Inductive reasoning is a skill that can be honed to razor sharpness, as witnessed by the exploits of one of my favorite characters, Sherlock Holmes.

- Reasonable facilities in communications, both written and oral, and in interpersonal relations. In the latter area, the planner must be equally comfortable and effective working as a member of a team or as an individual contributor.

- The ability to work in the shadow of the CEO, as opposed to being in the spotlight. As a corollary, recognition of accomplishments must frequently come from within the individual. The insecure person need not apply.

In contrast to most business disciplines, where measures of performance are concrete, visible and frequent, strategic planning is the most difficult of all functions to judge effectively. Its payoffs are frequently several years downstream, at a time when the particular projects have long since been disassociated from their progenitor.

As a case in point, several years ago I helped to establish at Storage Technology Corporation a new venture to manufacture internally the magnetic media used in our line of magnetic disk drives. (Theretofore, the company had purchased these media from external suppliers.) Toward this end, I screened several external entrepreneurs who approached the company, selected the best qualified, assisted him in developing a comprehensive strategic plan for the business, identified the key performance milestones by which we would measure progress, formulated an incentive compensation arrangement based on these milestones, negotiated the relevant contracts and obtained the CEO's approval of the deal.

Of course, in my capacity as chief strategic planner, I monitored the progress of this media operation over the ensuing months, but never had the occasion to visit the facility, which was located some 1000 miles from company headquarters. Two years later, I visited our media plant as a side trip to another appointment in the area. By that time, the operation had been fully integrated into the engineering and manufacturing operations of our company. My tour of the plant revealed an extremely clean, efficient and highly automated operation which, by that time, was producing disk media which were comparable in quality to any on the open market.

You can imagine my sense of pride at having spawned in the abstract two years earlier that which I now saw in the concrete. My recognition and reward came from within. More importantly, I was content with that. So it is with strategic planning. Others usually get the credit for finishing what you started. If that bothers you, I suggest that you try another line of work.

INTRODUCING INTERNATIONAL MICROWIDGETS

As I mentioned earlier, this book contains numerous excerpts from strategic plans of actual companies. The spectrum of companies ranges from start-ups to companies with decades of operating history, from small companies with revenues in the million-dollar range to giants with billions of dollars of revenues, and from splendid examples of success to abject failures. In each case, I have attempted to select an example that best illustrates the points that I am trying to make at that stage in the preparation of the strategic plan.

The flip side of using excerpts from actual plans is that, of the scores of strategic plans that I have authored or reviewed in my career, not one of them could serve in its entirety as a model for the relevant points that are presented in this book. For the most part, they are too long and detailed, which tends to obscure the simplicity and elegance of a thoughtfully prepared strategic plan. Just as you may be preparing a plan for your business as you are reading this book, so also will we prepare a plan, step by step, as we progress through the chapters of this book.

So, let me introduce you to our company, International Microwidgets. True, it is a fictitious company, but you will find that it, its competitors and the environment in which they operate reflect and are even remindful of circumstances in the real world of business. Let me give you a little background on the company.

As we all know, widgets have been manufactured since the dawn of the industrial revolution. According to my dictionary, widgets are small mechanical devices or controls. (A second definition also suggests that they are hypothetical manufactured articles, but we shall overlook that point for our purposes.) My dictionary is clearly obsolete, because in this era of the microprocessor, mechanical widgets have been supplanted by electronics widgets, or microwidgets. Let me describe the beginning of this revolution in widgetry.

In the early 1960's, a young French national by the name of William Portes emigrated from his native Algeria to study Electrical Engineering at the University of Pennsylvania in Philadelphia. William (or Bill, as he would be known to his many American friends) was attracted to Pennsylvania by its rich heritage in computer technology, for it was at the University of Pennsylvania that the world's first electronic digital computer, ENIAC, was born in 1946.

An acronym for Electronic Numerical Integrator and Calculator, ENIAC was a dinosaur by modern standards. It weighed 30 tons, contained 17,000 vacuum tubes, filled an entire room, consumed 150 kilowatts of power, and stored only 80 bytes of information. Today, computers in children's toys are thousands of times more powerful than ENIAC was.

But, ENIAC shortened the amount of time for the Army to compute ballistic firing tables from 12 hours, with mechanical calculators, to 30 seconds, a performance improvement of 1500 times. And, ENIAC ushered in the age of the electronic computer. ENIAC's lineal descendent was Univac, and fierce competition in the computer industry gave impetus to such companies as Burroughs, NCR, Control Data, Honeywell and, of course, IBM.

Plan For Profitability!

By the time that Bill Portes arrived at the University, the vacuum tube had given way to semiconductor technology, viz., the transistor. Enterprising semiconductor companies were beginning to experiment with prototypes of microchips, where several transistors were combined into a single package. Of course, as we all know, semiconductor technology would ultimately progress to packaging densities with hundreds, thousands and eventually millions of transistors packed onto a chip the size of a postage stamp.

Upon his graduation from Pennsylvania in the mid-1960's, Portes went to work for General Widgets, then the largest manufacturer of widgets in the world. Located in the Detroit area, General Widgets and two other manufacturers in the same area had long dominated the market for widgets. At that time, widgets were still totally mechanical devices since it had been impractical to incorporate vacuum tube or even discrete transistor electronics into the small forms of widgets.

With entrepreneurial foresight that would epitomize the rest of his career, Bill Portes anticipated the extensive potential of the microchip, and his vision was the motivation behind the decision to join General Widgets. He foresaw a time in the future when the nascent microchip would attain sufficient capability in performance that it could be incorporated into the form factor of the widget and, in the process, improve the functionality of the staid widget and open the door to numerous new applications and markets for the device.

Unfortunately for him, General Widgets (as well as the other two members of the big three) were comfortable and complacent with their dominant market shares and not inclined to accept such ideas of radical change. After

17

five years with General Widgets, Bill resigned to pursue his vision. The parting was amicable and Bill's future plans were fully supported by General Widgets, which, while being skeptical of the likelihood of his success, reasoned that, even if Portes was able to sell a few "microwidgets," he would buy the basic components from his former employer.

Bill Portes relocated to Boulder, Colorado, a burgeoning locale for high-technology start-up companies. To obtain the requisite capital to fund his new company, which he called International Microwidgets, he developed a strategic business plan and presented it to several venture capital companies, one of which saw the same potential for the project as did Bill and agreed to make an equity investment in the fledgling company.

The new company was launched in the early 1970's and turned a profit in its second full year of operation. In the mid-1970's, the company was growing so rapidly that its demand for capital to fund this growth had exceeded that which could be generated from private sources and from reinvested profits. Accordingly, the company turned to the public equity market with an initial public offering in 1975.

Today, International Microwidgets is the leader in the worldwide market for microwidgets, which have totally obsoleted mechanical widgets in much the same way that electronic calculators made mechanical and electromechanical calculators extinct. We shall learn more about this dynamic company as we develop its strategic business plan over the course of this book.

SUMMARY

If you are reading this book for enlightenment, please read on. However, if you need to write a strategic plan, I strongly recommend that you attempt a first pass of the subject of each chapter immediately after reading the chapter.

So, your task now is to decide whether your company consists of a single SBU or multiple SBU's. If your company is small, it is probably a single SBU. If large, it could consist of more than one SBU. To help you decide, recall that an SBU has:

- A homogeneous set of products or services;

- A quantifiable market with an identifiable set of competitors;

- An operating statement and a balance sheet.

A separate strategic plan is need for each SBU. In view of the amount of work required to prepare a strategic plan, it is sensible not to define any more strategic business units than are absolutely necessary.

CHAPTER II

THE STRUCTURE OF A STRATEGIC PLAN

"Begin at the beginning," the King said, gravely, "and go till you come to the end; then stop."
> Lewis Carroll, Alice's Adventures in Wonderland, 1865

You can never plan the future by the past.
> Edmund Burke, 1791

In preparing for battle I have always found that plans are useless, but planning is indispensable.
> Dwight D. Eisenhower, quoted by Richard Nixon in 1962

In the first chapter, I introduced the notion that strategic business planning is often accomplished as a staff extension of one of the many responsibilities of the Chief Executive Officer. The commitment of the CEO to the need for and the use of a strategic plan for his company is vital. It must be his plan for the company, not merely a document prepared by the staff as an annual exercise in form for the benefit of the company's top executives and the Board of Directors. If, in fact, the CEO is the ultimate formulator of company strategy, then the strategic plan must be the documentation of his strategy.

One of the most well known (and controversial) CEO's of the twentieth century firmly believed that "a [CEO's] correct ... decisions stem from his correct judgments, and his correct judgments stem from thorough and necessary [research]. ... He applies all the possible and necessary [research] and ponders on the information gathered about the [competitive] situation, discarding the dross and selecting the essential, eliminating the false and retaining the true, proceeding from the one to the other and from the outside to the inside. Then he takes the conditions on his own side into account, and makes a study of both sides and their interrelations, thereby forming his judgments, making up his mind and working out his plans. Such is the complete process of knowing a situation which a [CEO] goes through before he formulates a strategic plan."

The substitutions in the brackets are mine. The somewhat stilted construction is probably a result of the translation from the CEO's native language. The foregoing passage was lifted from the writings of the Mao Zedong. Lest you protest that the military parallel is inappropriate, it should be noted that the word *strategy* has its roots in the Latin word *strategein*, which translates roughly into *to lead an army*.

In this chapter, we shall explore the process by which a strategic plan is developed in a company and the resulting structure of the plan. In reality, no two companies do anything exactly the same way and strategic planning is no exception. Accordingly, the process and structure described in this book should be viewed as an amalgamation of my experience with many companies and even more strategic plans.

21

Lee E. Hargrave, Jr.

THE ANNUAL PLANNING CYCLE

At the outset, you must understand the difference between strategic planning and operational planning. The most obvious difference between the two is the span of time under consideration in the two plans. Strategic plans typically have planning horizons of from three to ten years, depending primarily upon the character of the businesses in which the company is engaged. Operational plans, on the other hand, usually focus on the fiscal year ahead. Since it is far easier to project measurable events six months in the future than six years out, operational plans involve substantially more precision and detail than do strategic plans.

For this discussion, let me assume that we are dealing with a company that has multiple SBU's. If your situation is that of a single SBU, then just disregard my comments about the competition among the SBU's for their shares of company resources.

A typical company strategic planning cycle is displayed in bar chart format in Figure 2-1. The approach to both the strategic plan and the operational plan consists conceptually of four steps, as follows:

- Assessment and identification of the issues that face the company. Examples of strategic issues include entry into new markets, the emergence of foreign competition, the effect of economic cycles on the business of the company, major shifts in strategies for key businesses, and so on. By contrast, operational issues deal with the more immediate concerns of the year ahead, such as the introduction of a new product, quarterly earnings, major capital expenditures, inventory levels, and the like. The key issues essentially provide both a perspective and a framework around which the strategic or operational plan is developed.

- Preparation and issuance of guidelines for preparing the plan. Any plan that is truly representative of the entire company requires coordinated contributions from all of the organizational components of the company. The guidelines spell out what is expected of each contributing organization and when it is expected.

- The actual preparation of the plan. This is usually an iterative process, because seldom do the sum of the initial plans of the SBU's result in a satisfactory company plan. What usually transpires are several cycles of top-down direction from the CEO and subsequent bottom-up responses from the SBU's, with the process homing in on a company plan that reconciles the collective aspirations of the SBU's with the finite resources of the company as a whole.

- Clearly, the process of preparing the plan inherently encompasses substantial internal review and approval. In fact, if the CEO is actively involved in the preparation (as should be the case), review and approval by the full-time management of the company is accomplished as the plan is prepared. Nevertheless, after the plan has been prepared, there is frequently a formal session with top management and the Board of Directors at which time the plan is presented to all concerned and formally approved.

As shown in Figure 2-1, the strategic plan precedes the operational plan. Of importance, the first year of the strategic plan represents a foundation upon which the more detailed operational plan for the ensuing fiscal year is developed.

Figure 2-1
The Annual Corporate Planning Cycle

There are some companies that develop both plans in parallel, but my experience is that the parallel approach runs the risk of producing an inferior strategic plan. Given the choice of evaluating the effect of concrete events in the year ahead or the vague expectations of several years in the future, the human tendency is to focus on the former at the expense of the latter. For this reason, I prefer (and most companies follow) the serial planning approach displayed in Figure 2-1.

Plan For Profitability!

THE PLANNING HORIZON

One of the initial decisions that confronts each SBU that intends to prepare a strategic plan is how many years into the future can be realistically predicted. Although five years is the most commonly encountered strategic planning horizon, there is no single absolute horizon that fits all businesses. The choice of planning horizon depends largely upon the response time of the markets that the SBU serves, i.e., the time lag between present actions and their response and full impact at some time in the future.

As a general rule, the larger the capital investment associated with an SBU's strategic actions, the longer the time until results can be expected, ergo the longer the planning horizon. For example, SBU's involved in such industries as aerospace, petrochemicals and nuclear energy may require planning horizons as long as 20 years. To the other extreme, retailers and service-oriented businesses cannot realistically expect to forecast their future beyond three years.

Since the strategic plan of a company is the sum of the strategic plans of its SBU's, it follows that the company's planning horizon is restricted to the shortest planning horizon among its SBU's. As mentioned previously, five years is the most prevalent duration, and I have used five years in most of the examples in this book.

Coupled with the question of how far into the future the strategic plan should project is the allied question of how far into the past the plan should cover. In other words, how many years of historical data should be contained in the plan?

25

The need for historical information may not be readily apparent to the reader. If so, consider the projection displayed in Figure 2-2, where profits are projected to rise steadily from this year (year zero) over the next five years.

Figure 2-2
A Profit Forecast

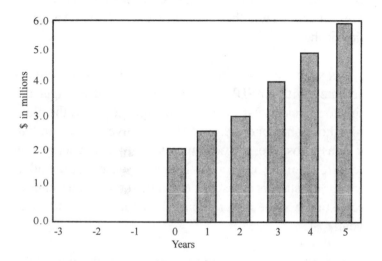

Figure 2-2 appears to be a favorable forecast, and indeed it is if the profits of prior years are as pictured in Figure 2-3. However, if the profit history is that of Figure 2-4, the profit forecast should be a cause for considerable concern for the CEO.

In short, a few years of historical data provide a frame of reference for the projections of the strategic plan, with particular emphasis on spotting favorable or unfavorable trends. Again, there is no fixed rule for how many years of history to cover in the plan. My personal preference is for the plan to look backward about half as many years as it looks forward. Thus, a five-year plan would contain three years of history, as depicted in the examples of Figures 2-2 through 2-4.

Figure 2-3
Favorable Trend

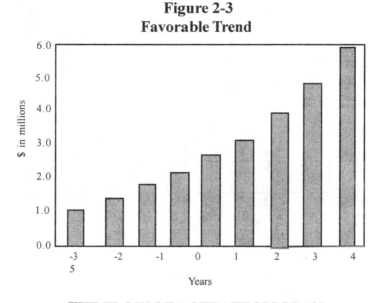

THE FLOW OF A STRATEGIC PLAN

In succeeding chapters, we shall explore the essential elements of a strategic plan for an individual SBU. These elements are displayed in the flow diagram of Figure 2-5, which depicts the primary dependencies that exist in the preparation of the plan.

Preparing a strategic plan is, in itself, a highly iterative process. Completion of each element of the plan entails going back to prior elements and fine-tuning or otherwise adjusting them to conform to what has followed. No attempt has been made to display all of these iterative feedback loops in the flow chart of Figure 2-5.

27

Figure 2-4
Unfavorable Trend

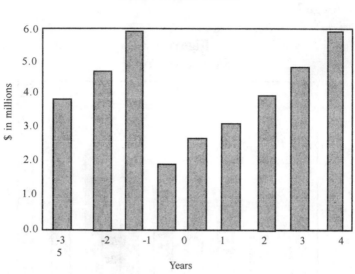

In brief, the major elements of a strategic plan should attempt to answer the following questions:

● *Mission*: What is the purpose of the SBU? Why is it in business?

● *Market:* What is the size of the market that the SBU serves (or plans to serve)? How is it expected to change over the planning horizon, and why?

● *Competition:* Who are the major competitors? What are their strengths and weaknesses? What shares of the market do they command? What strategies are they believed to be following?

- *Self-Evaluation:* Likewise, what are our SBU's strengths and weaknesses? What is our market share?

- *Opportunities and Threats:* What opportunities exist (or are likely to exist during the planning period) upon which the SBU can capitalize? What threats must be countered?

Figure 2-5
The Flow of a Strategic Plan

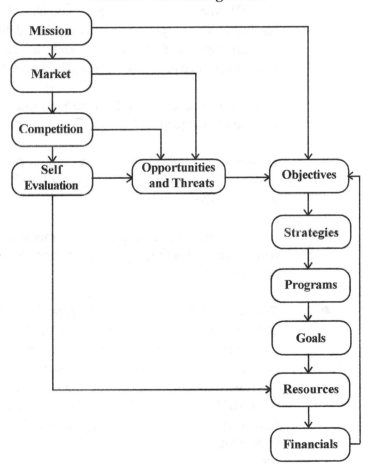

Opportunities and threats are situations which arise from the analysis of the *environment,* which may be divided into the external and the internal environment. The *external* environment is that over which the SBU has little control, viz., the market and the competition. The *internal* environment is that within the SBU itself, over which we should have a high degree of control.

- *Objectives*: Broadly, what should the SBU attempt to accomplish over the planning horizon? The SBU's objectives must be framed against the back drop of reality in terms of what should be accomplished (the SBU's mission) and what can be accomplished (the opportunities and threats).

- *Strategies*: Broadly, how does the SBU intend to achieve its objectives?

- *Programs*: Specifically, what measurable activities does the SBU plan to initiate (or continue) to implement its strategies?

- *Goals*: By what specific quantitative measures will the SBU track the progress and performance of its programs?

- *Resources*: What people, facilities, equipment and funds are required to carry out the plan? The answer to this question often results in a major iteration back through the preceding elements of the flow shown in Figure 2-5. This is because most SBU's have limited resources and cannot fund all of the programs that they would like to undertake.

Plan For Profitability!

- *Financials*: What revenues and profits can be expected to result from the straregic plan? How will funds be generated and used? What sort of balance sheets can be expected?

In the remainder of this chapter and in subsequent chapters, we will explore each of the foregoing questions and, in the process, demonstrate how a strategic plan is developed.

THE MISSION

I have observed that the first step in preparing a strategic plan, that of defining and documenting the mission of the company or SBU, is also the most frequently omitted step in the process. When this is the case, one of two underlying conditions exists.

One of these is when the CEO or General Manager has such a clear idea of the purpose of his business that he assumes that the mission is self-evident to everyone in the organization. In reality, the clarity of the mission diminishes rapidly as one descends down the organizational chain of command. I have attended numerous strategy sessions with second- and third-level managers that degraded into their plaintive discourses on the need for a better understanding of the CEO's view of the purpose of the company. The moral of this situation is: if the mission is known, write it down so that everyone concerned understands it.

At the other extreme is the more serious situation where no one is really quite sure of the purpose of the company. At first thought, this situation may appear to be so remote as to be ludicrous, but I have encountered more than one

CEO who could not cogently articulate the purpose of his company.

The mission of a company depends upon the CEO's value structure and his perception of the values of customers, shareholders and employees. The mission statement is the foundation upon which the rest of the strategic plan is developed. It establishes the general direction in which the company should be headed. Of note, the mission statement may be reshaped and refined by the understanding that results as the rest of the strategic plan is developed.

Although the mission statement is the shortest element of the strategic plan, it is far from the easiest to develop. Many people find it far easier to jump into quantifying the served market (Chapter III) than to synthesize the mission statement from perceptions and observations.

To catalyze the process, I find it helpful to address three questions:

1) What are the present characteristics of the business?

2) What differentiates the business from its competitors?

3) What would we like to see the business become in the future?

MISSION STATEMENTS

To illustrate the process of developing the mission, let me offer some examples of well written mission statements, starting with one of the classic case studies in business school literature, the Head Ski Company.[1] This case involves

32

Plan For Profitability!

Howard Head's development and introduction of his revolutionary metal ski from the founding of the company in 1950 through 1968. A mission statement for the Head Ski Company might have read as follows:

> As a high-quality and innovative producer and supplier of metal skis, serving the high-priced end of the ski market; with unique capabilities to design and build metal skis, a reputation for innovation and leadership in this market, and particular appeal to young, affluent, recreational consumers in the United States: the Head Ski Company intends to maintain its image as a quality producer and to expand its products and services into areas that are compatible with its abilities and strengths.

Note that the Head Ski Company mission statement addresses the prior three questions in a concise and straightforward manner. It practically points the way for Head's post-1968 expansion into expensive ski- and sportswear, fiberglass skis and tennis rackets.

---

[1] C.Roland Christiansen et al, Business Policy, Richard C. Irwin, Homewood, Illinois, 1982

The mission of Mitsubishi Electric circa 1985 was constructed along similar lines:

> Mitsubishi Electric Corporation is a full-range manufacturer of electrical and electronic equipment, from giant power generators to compact home appliances. Since our founding in 1921, we have become one of Japan's leading manufacturers in this field. Based upon this experience, we are actively pursuing technological research that will contribute to the development and progress of societies throughout the world.[2]

For another example, the following is the mission of Storage Technology Corporation circa 1983:

> Storage Technology Corporation designs, manufactures, distributes and services high-performance magnetic tape and disk storage subsystems and high-speed line printers to leading users and original equipment manufacturers throughout the world. Founded in 1969, Storage Technology is recognized for the price-performance advantages of its equipment and for its substantial shares of the markets it serves. Storage Technology plans to continue to offer its customers the latest in advanced-technology peripherals for high-performance data processing systems.

---

[2] Undated publication of Mitsubishi Electric Corporation

Plan For Profitability!

In 1983, Advanced Pumping Systems Inc. was a developmental-stage company that was attempting to penetrate the market for oil well pumping units. Here is their articulation of their mission:

> Advanced Pumping Systems (APS) designs and markets universally adaptable oil pumping units to oil industry customers in the United States. Founded in 1981, APS is an innovator in the design of oil pumping equipment with distinctive operational simplicity, versatility, and cost effectiveness. Three APS pumping units have been designed to handle the full range of gear requirements that previously required ten times as many different-sized conventional units. In addition, APS has designed technically innovative oil well simulation and analysis equipment that can provide accurate performance data on its competitors' units as well as its own. APS plans to stay at the leading edge of pumping unit design by implementing remote monitoring capabilities to existing units and by designing a highly advanced electronic pumping unit that should revolutionize the industry.

All four of the foregoing examples have the hallmarks of well-conceived mission statements. They are concise, sufficiently explicit to exclude those business areas for which the companies are clearly not suited, yet sufficiently flexible to permit expansion into areas that are compatible with the companies' experiences and strengths.

THE MISSION OF INTERNATIONAL
MICROWIDGETS

As you will recall, we introduced International Microwidgets in the last chapter and mentioned that the company had the leading share of the worldwide market for widgets. Since we will discuss the size of the widget market and of International Microwidgets' share in the next two chapters, we will defer market quantification until then. Of interest, though, is that the company is also the lowest cost producer of microwidgets in this fiercely cost-competitive market. It frequently follows that the market leader is also the lowest-cost producer according to the principle of the learning curve, which we will cover in Chapter V.

Remember that the are three questions, the answers to which frame a concise statement of a company's mission. The first question is:

What are the present characteristics of the business?

Faced with this question, Bill Portes, the President and CEO of International Microwidgets, answers it in one succinct sentence, as follows:

International Microwidgets is the largest and lowest-cost producer of microwidgets in the world.

The second of the three questions is:

What differentiates the business from its competitors?

Now, of course, being the market leader and the lowest-cost producer both qualify as answers to this question, but Portes opts to highlight these attributes in his opening sentence. To answer the second question, he goes straight to the point:

> The company is universally recognized as the inventor of the microwidget and a pioneer in expanding the applications of microwidgets to diverse markets.

An entrepreneur like Portes typically has to be constrained in limiting his answers to the third question, which, as you will recall, is:

> What would we like to see the business be come in the future?

Like any effective CEO, Portes's list of projects for improving the positioning of the company is long, but he chooses to highlight only his two top concerns in the mission statement. One of these is the issue of geographical market coverage, which is weak in Asia, particularly in the emerging market of China, and in Eastern Europe, notably in the former Soviet Union. A Japanese competitor has a commanding lead in cultivating the Chinese market, while a German competitor dominates the former Russian states. Since these are the two highest growth segments of the global market, decisive steps need to be taken to improve the company's positioning there.

Another issue is that of maintaining low-cost production. Portes has discerned a disturbing trend in manufacturing costs over the past two years, in that their rate of decline appears to be leveling off. He recognizes that two major steps need to be taken if the company is to maintain its cost advantage over its competitors: (1) integrating more vertically by manufacturing microchips in house rather than sourcing them from vendors and (2) moving certain manufacturing operations to lower-cost sites offshore.

These programs resulting from these high-level concerns are elaborated upon in the Programs section of the strategic plan, which we will develop in Chapter VI. In the mission statement, the CEO sets the stage for these major program thrusts by simply stating:

> The company intends to maintain its worldwide leadership by creatively continuing to improve the affordability of its products and by aggressively positioning its products as the products of choice throughout the world.

Putting these three elements together, we have the mission statement of International Microwidgets and the forerunner for the rest of the strategic plan:

> International Microwidgets is the largest and lowest-cost producer of microwidgets in the world. The company is universally recognized as the inventor of the microwidget and a pioneer in expanding the applications of microwidgets to diverse markets. The company intends to maintain its leadership by creatively continuing to improve the affordability of its products and by aggressively positioning its products as the products of choice throughout the world.

Plan For Profitability!

SUMMARY

The preferred planning cycle for a company is to prepare the strategic plan in the first half of the fiscal year and the more detailed operational plan in the second half. Such a cycle permits the planners to focus on strategic issues independently of operational issues and vice versa. Once the strategic plan is completed, the data for the first year of the strategic plan establishes a framework for the operational plan.

Both planning cycles have four sequential steps:

- Identification of key issues;

- Guidelines for preparing the plan;

- Preparation of the plan;

- Review and approval.

At the outset of the strategic planning process, one of the first decisions that needs to be made is the forward time span, or planning horizon, of the plan. Most companies employ a planning horizon of five years. For a five-year plan, it is also useful to include historical data for the previous three years so that trends can be spotted easily.

There are 11 sequential elements to a strategic business plan: mission, market, competition, self-evaluation, opportunities and threats, objectives, strategies, programs, goals, resources and financials. Although the elements are inherently sequential, the process is highly iterative; as each downstream element is completed, prior upstream elements are frequently revised.

The first step in the preparation of the strategic plan is to define the mission of the company. The mission statement should answer three questions:

- What are the present characteristics of the business?

- What differentiates the business from its competitors?

- What would we like to see the business become in the future?

So, if you are preparing a strategic plan for your company for the first time, your next step is to write the mission statement. Give it a try, using the four mission statements cited earlier in this chapter as examples. I also suggest that you forego attempting perfection at this time because you will probably fine-tune the mission statement as you work through the other elements of the strategic plan.

CHAPTER III

THE MARKET

The market came with the dawn of civilization and it is not an invention of capitalism.

Mikhail Gorbachev, 1990

There are three kinds of lies: lies, damned lies and statistics.

Benjamin Disraeli, quoted by Charles Neider, 1959

I will stand on, and continue to use, the figures I have used, because I believe they are correct. Now, I'm not going to deny that you don't now and then slip up on something; no one bats a thousand.

Ronald Reagan, 1980

Some years ago, I embarked upon the task of developing a strategic plan for the fledgling telecommunications subsidiary of my company. One of my first actions was to meet with the manager of planning and the manager of marketing of the subsidiary to begin to understand the market that they were attempting to enter. After all, I reasoned, who better should understand the market than these two people?

Their response to my first question indicated that my task was going to be far more difficult than I had originally thought. After the introductory pleasantries has been exchanged, I opened the discussion of the strategic plan by inquiring about the size of the market that they were attempting to serve with their first product. After a moment of blank stares, the planner responded, "It's huge."

In fact, they had no idea whether their market was closer to a million dollars or a billion dollars in annual placements. As it turned out, my analysis revealed that their market was relatively small in comparison to the markets of other businesses within the parent company. As an indirect consequence of this conclusion, I directed the divestiture of the subsidiary some three years later.

In preparing a strategic plan, the first step after articulating the mission of the business is to define and quantify the market in which the business will participate. In my experience, one of the two most prevalent reasons for the failure of new business ventures is the lack of adequate understanding of the market that the new company intends to serve. (The other reason is inadequate capitalization.)

I learned the importance of understanding the market the hard way. In the mid-1960's, I was president of a small company that was developing a portable machine to punch tabulating cards at the point of sale. At that time, punched cards were the primary means of entering data into computer systems. Our concept was to place these machines at the vendors' sites and capture the information in machine-readable punched-card form there, thus eliminating the laborious and expensive process of keypunching each transaction from sales slips at the company's central data processing site. The primary targets for our product were the oil companies, specifically, credit card transactions at service stations.

As a registered professional engineer, I can assure you

that our *source punch* was a well-designed product. The service station attendant merely inserted the customer's credit card, dialed in the amount of the sale, pulled the handle of the machine, and thus produced a punched card with a detachable stub receipt for the customer. We even engaged one of the leading industrial designers of the 1960's to design a stylish exterior for the product.

After two years of design and development, we began to preview our product before the leading oil companies in the United States. After a few months of intensive meetings with oil companies, the painful reality of the situation became evident. A competing technology, optical character recognition, was in the process of emerging from the laboratory into its first commercial applications. In effect, this new technology had aborted our product before we could even bring it to market.

With optical character recognition, all that was needed at the point of sale was an imprinter, a machine that was far less expensive than our source punch. The conversion from imprinted sales slips to machine language was performed automatically at the central data processing site by an optical scanner that recognized the imprinted characters and converted them into computer input code.

In short, we had failed to research the market for our product prior to expending development funds. We had designed a product for which there was a market that was disappearing. What a painful introduction to market research!

Of note, optical scanning was supplanted in the 1970's by direct-entry point-of-sale terminals. So the technological innovation that doomed our source punch was in turn doomed by another technological innovation. This exemplifies market *technology cycles*, which are discussed in this chapter.

THE SERVED MARKET

The moral of the foregoing story is that the SBU must define in unambiguous terms and then *quantify* the market that it serves or plans to serve. The adjective *served* is important, for seldom does a single company have the breadth of both product line and distribution to cover the entirety of its potential market. A company's served market is a subset of the total market for its products or services. An example may help to clarify this concept of the served market.

Consider a company that manufactures and markets typewriters. To be sure, I am well aware that no one manufactures typewriters anymore, but it turns out that the industrial designer whom I engaged to stylize our source punch also designed the then-famous Royal typewriter. In the process of working with him, I learned something about the typewriter market.

How does one begin to quantify a company's served market for typewriters? Let us begin with Figure 3-1.

At the outset, we can assume that the company's potential market is the total worldwide market for typewriters of all types. In reality, however, there was at the time no company in the world that manufactured every type of typewriter in use and also had the distribution network to reach every user of typewriters. So, we must divide the market into that portion which the company serves (the served market) and that which it does not. This can be done by asking a few straightforward

44

questions, such as:

- In what alphabets does the company manufacture its typewriters? In the example of Figure 3-1, our company manufactures only English-alphabet typewriters. Thus, in one stroke, we can exclude all other alphabets, among them Cyrillic, Arabic, Farsi, the many oriental character sets, and even Latin alphabets which have similarities to English (French, German, etc.).

- In what areas of the world does the company market its typewriters? In this example, our company has the resources to market only in North America, specifically, the United States, Mexico and Canada. Again, with one question, we can exclude three-quarters of the gross world product from our sphere of concern. Reflect also upon the fact that our company cannot serve two major alphabetic applications in North America: Spanish applications in Mexico and French applications in Canada.

- Does the company offer both manual and electric models? Our company of Figure 3-1 does not serve the manual market and offers only electric models.

- Does the company offer both portable and non-portable models? In this example, our company offers only non-portable models.

Lee E. Hargrave, Jr.

**Figure 3-1
Defining the Served Market**

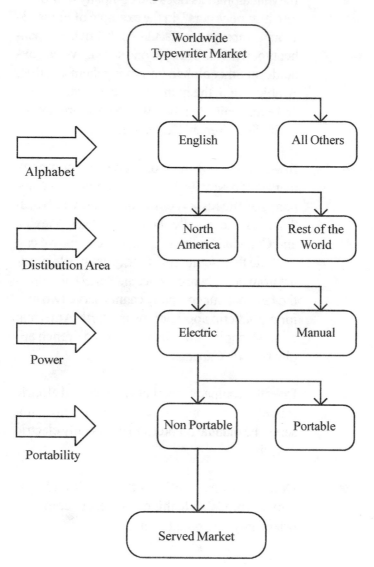

Plan For Profitability!

By a judicious line of questioning such as the foregoing, it is possible to define very precisely the market that a business serves. In our typewriter example, the served market is the North American market for non-portable, electric, English-alphabet typewriters, a market that was easily quantifiable (with research) to a reasonable degree of precision.

Here are a few examples of the numerous markets with which I have been concerned in my career:

- Printers: High-speed, impact, line printers (1200 lines per minute and above) in North and South America, Western Europe, North Africa, the Middle East, Japan and Australia.

- Spacecraft: The worldwide market for unmanned spacecraft that employ three-axis stabilization (in contrast to spin stabilization).

- Pumping Units: The worldwide market for production oil-well pumping units.

- Food Processors: The market in the United States, Canada and Western Europe for home food processors.

MARKET SEGMENTATION

Once the served market is defined, it is useful to *segment* the served market in a manner that aids in understanding the composition and dynamics of the market. Among the ways in which a market can be subdivided are by *geography*, *channel of distribution*, *product features or characteristics, product application or use,* and *purchaser characteristics.*

For example, our served market for typewriters (Figure 3-1) may be segmented in at least three ways, each of which provides insight into how the market is structured. Consider segmenting the market by:

- Geography
  - Canada
  - United States
  - Mexico

- Channel of distribution
  - Directly to customers
  - Through retailers
  - Through wholesalers or distributors

- Application
  - Home
  - Office

As another example, a manufacturer of personal deodorant for the U. S. market may elect to segment its served market as follows:

- Geography
  - Eastern Region: from Pittsburgh eastward
  - Western Region: west of the Rockies
  - Central Region: all that in between

- Channel of distribution
  - Food stores
  - Drug stores
  - Discount chains
  - All others

- Product characteristics
  - Spray
  - Roll-on
  - Stick

- Purchaser
  - Male
  - Female

In deciding how to segment the SBU's served market, it is important to make sure that the amount of effort required to obtain the segmented data is commensurate with the insight that the segmentation results provide. Each additional dimension of segmentation geometrically increases the size of the data. In general, it is safe to assume that, if one is in doubt whether to add another dimension of segmentation or not, it is probably best not to.

Again, some examples from my personal experience may be helpful. In the previous section, I cited four of the many markets in which I have been involved: printers, spacecraft, pumping units and food processors. I elected to segment each of these markets as follows:

Printers
- Performance
  - 1200-1800 lines per minute
  - Above 1800 lines per minute

- Distribution
    - Directly to printer users
    - To resellers
- Geography
    - United States
    - International

Spacecraft
Geographically by country

Pumping Units
- Performance
    - 114,000-320,000 inch-pounds torque
    - 320,000-912,000 inch-pounds torque
- Geography
    - United States
    - International

Food Processors
Geographically into the United States, Canada, France,
Germany and the rest of Western Europe

As I mentioned earlier, each added dimension into which
the served market is segmented has a geometrical effect
on the number of market data categories that must be obtained, which in turn compounds the complexity of gathering,
analyzing, understanding and presenting the data. To illustrate my point, consider again the typewriter market example.
If we had chosen to restrict our segmentation to a single dimension, say geography, there would have resulted only three
categories of data, as follows:

Plan For Profitability!

Geography
Canada
United States
Mexico

Adding the second dimension of the channel of distribution, which itself has three categories, increases the number of possible data categories to nine (3 x 3 = 9):

Geography	Distribution
Canada	Direct
United States	Retailers
Mexico	Distributors

In other words, each category in the first column can be combined with three categories in the second column, yielding a total of nine categories into which the served market data must be compartmentalized. Adding the third dimension of segmentation, application, compounds the complexity even further:

Geography	Distribution	Application
Canada	Direct	Office
United States	Retailers	Home
Mexico	Distributors	

Now there are 18 categories (3 x 3 x 2 = 18) into which we must sort our market data. This phenomenon of the geometrical expansion of market data categories is a good reason to use discretion in deciding how best to segment the served market under study.

Lee E. Hargrave, Jr.

SOURCES OF MARKET DATA

Undoubtedly the most challenging part of defining the SBU's market is that of obtaining the data, a process that is referred to as *market research*. I mentioned earlier that the material for this book began as a series of lecture notes to business school students. One of the lessons that I learned when I was teaching at the University of Colorado was that most of my students performed poorly in market research for assigned case studies or projects, simply because they were not sufficiently familiar with the relevant markets to know where to turn for reliable sources of historical data and projections. By contrast, the dedicated strategic planner is usually familiar with and has access to market information relevant to his business.

Another prevalent misconception of the business school students was that market research consisted primarily of contacting consumers in person or by telephone or mail and polling them as to their purchasing preferences. Introductory marketing textbooks sow the seeds of this misconception by presenting so many consumer market examples in their materials, and these seeds find fertile soil in the minds of the students who are themselves consumers, who have probably responded to market surveys, and who likely have never been directly exposed to non-consumer markets. In my business career, I have never personally conducted a market survey to obtain market data, although many of my sources of market data resulted from such surveys.

The point is that most planners use *secondary sources* of market data, as opposed to *primary sources*. Among frequently used secondary sources are government publications, statistical abstracts, business periodicals, trade journals, trade association publications, business research services, and the publications of consultants or other market specialists. Such secondary sources are so widely used simply because they are available, are less expensive than market research, and can be tapped in far less time than that required to gather data from primary sources.

Of course, someone ultimately has to tap the primary sources, and that someone could well be the strategic planner if the market data that he requires is not available from secondary sources. The advantages of sourcing primary data are that the data obtained can be tailored to the planner's requirements and that the data is proprietary to the company and may give the company an edge over its competitors. More often that not, however, the planner will have neither the time nor the personnel to conduct the research and will contract the task to an organization that specializes in such assignments.

QUANTIFYING THE MARKET

The appropriate measurement for quantifying the served market is usually readily apparent to those who are involved in the business of the SBU. It is usually either a measurement of *units* or of *dollars* (or any other currency that is a relevant measure).

For example, consider a company that distributes potatoes at wholesale to the domestic market. (For the record, this is one business in which I have absolutely no experience.) Our potato company should be primarily interested in the number of pounds (or tons) of potatoes that are consumed in the United States on an annual basis. This is a *units* orientation.

To be sure, our wholesaler is vitally concerned with the price of potatoes, since the price ultimately determines its margin of profit. However, there is little price differentiation among potatoes (of the same variety) at any point in time and the distributor measures its participation in the market by its poundage of shipments versus that of the total market. Year-to-year comparisons of the total market poundage provides insight into whether the market is declining, level or growing, whereas such comparison of the dollar volume of the market does not provide such insight unless it is accompanied by a tabulation of the annual price of potatoes.

To the other extreme, service-oriented businesses such as advertising agencies are primarily concerned with the *dollars* that are available for their services over a period of time. Since there are wide variations among the rates that advertising agencies charge for their services and among the usage charges of the diverse advertising media, there is no single unit of measurement other than dollars that adequately quantifies the market.

In the majority of situations, it is instructive to quantify the served market in terms of *both* units and dollars, especially when there are significant changes over time in the price per unit.

When I was teaching, at this point in the discussion of the market, one of the brighter students in my class would inevitably bring up the subject of inflation and the allied question of whether the market should be quantified in *constant dollars* or in *current dollars*. You will recall that constant dollars are expressed in terms of a base year (e.g., 1980 dollars) and exclude the effects of inflation. Current dollars, as their name suggests, represent the actual value of the dollar each year and include the effects of inflation.

Plan For Profitability!

My preference is to express all dollar values throughout the strategic plan, beginning with the market data, in terms of current dollars. Remember that the final products of the strategic plan (see Figure 2-5) are historical and projected financial statements, and business people are accustomed to viewing such exhibits in current dollars, not in constant dollars. Accordingly, I prefer to start with current dollars and employ them consistently throughout the plan. Regardless of whether the choice is to use current or constant dollars, the issue of inflation must be addressed squarely in either case, because the underlying assumptions regarding inflation must be articulated at the outset of the strategic plan.

As an example, suppose that unit prices are predicated to rise by 5% per year over the horizon of the strategic plan. This means that a constant dollar in the fifth year of the plan equates to slightly less than $1.28 in current dollars in the same year (because of the effect of compound interest). If current dollars are used in the plan, this 5% inflation assumption must be stated at the outset so that it can be factored into unit cost and price analyses. If, on the other hand, the plan employs constant dollars throughout, then the 5% inflation rate assumption must also be identified so that the reader can convert constant dollars to current dollars if he wishes to do so.

MARKET MEASUREMENTS

The most obvious descriptors of a market are its *size* and its rate of *growth* (or decline). Size is a relative indicator, since a market can be described as large or small only when it is compared to other markets, such as the served markets of other SBU's within the parent company.

Growth can be expressed in terms of the average annual percentage rate by which the market changes over the forecast period, taking into account the effect of compounding. Thus, a market with an average growth rate of 14% per year will double itself in about five years. One that is declining by 10% per year will be half its initial size in seven years. In planning literature, these market growth percentages are often referred to by the initials CGR (compound growth rate) or AAG (average annual growth).

You do not need a computer, a calculator or a compound interest table to be convinced that 14% translates into a doubling cycle of approximately five years or that 10% yields a cycle of about seven years. These results can be derived mentally by using the *Rule of 70,* an excellent tool for the strategic planner to have at his disposal. Simply put, the Rule of 70 states that the multiplicative product of growth (or decline) rate in percent and the number of years it takes the market to double (or halve) is approximately equal to 70. In the above examples, 14 x 5 = 70 and 10 x 7 = 70.

The Rule of 70 is an approximation and does not yield exact results. The error increases as AAG increases (i.e., when the doubling period is short), and this error factor is shown by the graph of Figure 3-2. For a doubling period of two years, for example, the Rule of 70 suggests that the growth rate should be 35%, whereas the correct value is 41%. In general, the Rule of 70 is reasonably accurate for periods greater than two years.

Figure 3-2
Rule of 70

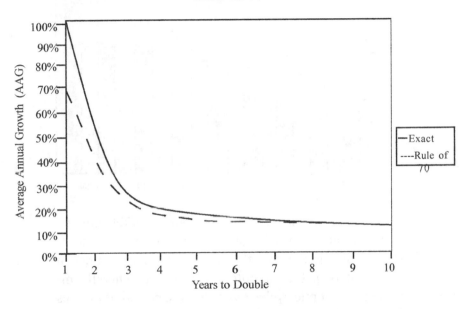

CHRONOLOGICAL MARKET DATA

Markets are seldom so regular that they increase or decrease so as to replicate faithfully the textbook examples of compound principal and interest. Consider the example of Figures 3-3 and 3-4, which are from my personal planning files and are vintage 1981. They depict the worldwide market for high-performance mainframe computers in equivalent annual sales (dollar terms) and in annual shipments (unit terms), respectively.

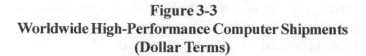

Figure 3-3
Worldwide High-Performance Computer Shipments
(Dollar Terms)

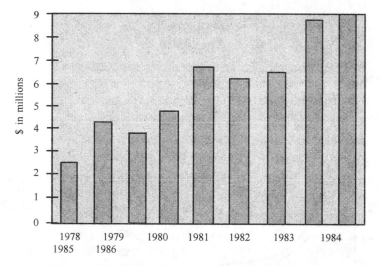

Although it is clear that the computer market depicted in these figures is growing at a healthy rate, note that there are two dips in the growth, one in 1980 and another in 1983. Although the computer business was generally immune to economic cycles over the time period of Figures 3-3 and 3-4, computers had their own intrinsic cycles of technological obsolescence, whereby one generation of machines was replaced a few years later by a successor generation employing more advanced technology. The slight downturns in 1980 and 1983 are the result of users' deferrals of machine purchases in anticipation of the availability of next-generation machines.

Unless the data is in an awful mess, however, I prefer merely to find that percentage rate which compounds the initial year's value (e.g., $2.3 billion in Figure 3-3) into the final year's value ($9.0 billion), which is a rudimentary calculation on most personal computers. By this simplistic approach, the AAG's turn out to be 19% and 14% for Figures 3-3 and 3-4, respectively, which represents an error of at most one part in eight from the more precise values.

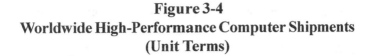

Figure 3-4
Worldwide High-Performance Computer Shipments
(Unit Terms)

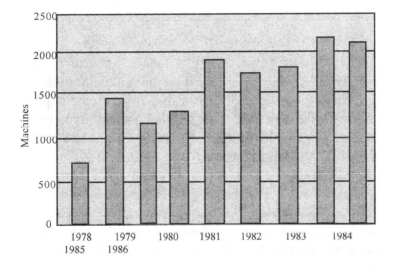

If you are uneasy in accepting this approximation, you are missing the point. Whether the AAG of Figure 3-3 is 17% or 19% is immaterial. The material point is that the market of Figure 3-3 exhibits robust growth, and an error of one part in eight is certainly less than the accuracy with which we can predict any market five years in the future.

As an aside, the reader may be curious as to why the average price per machine increases slightly over the eight-year time span of Figures 3-3 and 3-4. In 1978 it amounts to $3.2 million per machine ($2.3 billion divided by 723 machines), while in 1986 it is $4.2 million per machine ($9.0 billion divided by 2130 machines). In high-technology businesses such as computers, the expectation is that technological advances will more than offset inflation and will tend to drive unit prices down, and this would not appear to be the case in this example. What the data of these figures does not show is that the average computing power of a machine nearly tripled over the period from 1978 to 1986, so that the price per unit of computing power declined sharply over the period.

By way of another example, Figure 3-5 depicts the worldwide market for oil-well pumping units (within a specified range of pumping capacities) over the time span from 1978 through 1988. Note that the company segmented the data geographically into only two segments: the United States and the rest of the world.

This data was generated in 1983, which implies that the company chose to employ a planning horizon of five years, as well as five years of historical data. That makes 11 years in all: five historical (1978-82), five forecast (1984-88) and the current year (1983).

The most reliable of these three sets of data is, of course, the historical set, which we shall henceforth annotate with an (A) for actual data to connote that it is the most accurate data of the three sets. The most conjectural set of data is the market forecast, particularly in the out years; this set of data is denoted with an (F) for forecast data.

Figure 3-5
Worldwide Market for Oil-Well Pumping Units

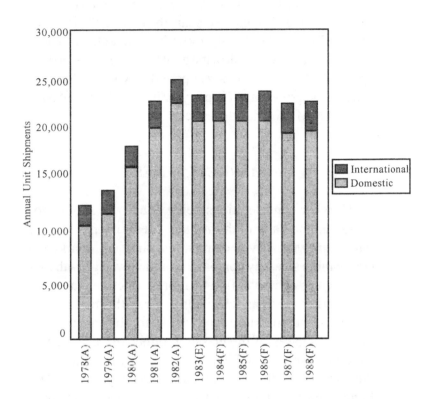

Which leads us to the question of how to characterize the data for the year in which the plan was generated, in this case, 1983. Recall from Chapter II (Figure 2-1) that the strategic plan is usually generated in the first half of the SBU's fiscal year, ideally in the second quarter. At that point in time some of the data is firm since a few months of the year have already elapsed, but the data for the entire year are several months from being actual data. We shall use an (E) for estimated data to describe the nature of the data in the year in which the strategic plan is prepared. Note these designations on the horizontal yearly axis of Figure 3-5.

Observe also from Figure 3-5 that worldwide shipments grow from 11,500 pumping units in 1978 to 25,100 units in 1988. Since this represents slightly more than doubling the market over this ten-year span, the rule of 70 yields that the AAG should be slightly above 7%. In fact, it is 8%. In this example, however, all of the growth occurs in the first five years (1978-83) of the ten-year period. I would rather characterize the growth as 17% per year from 1978 to 1983 and essentially a flat market thereafter.

MARKET CYCLES

All other considerations being equal, the single most important indicator of the attractiveness of a market is its rate of growth. Given comparable shares of markets of comparable size, any company would view a growth market (such as computers) to be more attractive than a mature market (such as television). Growth, maturity and decline are familiar terms, of course, for they are the three principal phases of the classic product life cycle curve, which is displayed in Figure 3-6. Simply put, the farther the market is to the left on the evolutionary time scale of Figure 3-6, the more attractive it is because of its potential for growth.

There are other cycles that are relevant in the analysis of market data and in spotting (or predicting) trends. Paramount among these are economic cycles of growth and recession. Mature markets that are serviced by discretionary capital are particularly vulnerable to economic cycles. Examples include machine tools, automobiles and housing.

Governmental influence can also play a major role in

shaping trends in certain markets, or even in creating some markets. As a case in point, clean air legislation in the early 1970's virtually created the market for air pollution equipment. Government regulation and deregulation can choke down or rapidly expand markets in short order. Federal defense policies can portend boom or bust for the contractors that participate in the defense market. These are but a few examples.

**Figure 3-6
The Concept of Product Life Cycle**

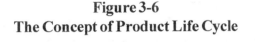

Growth   Maturity   Decline

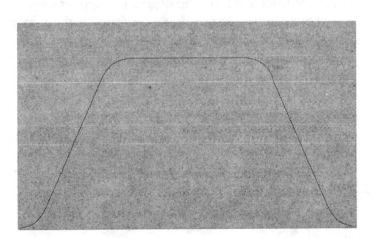

Time

In a society that is becoming increasingly dependent upon technology, technological cycles, which were almost unheard of in the literature 40 years ago, are increasingly important. The computer example of Figures 3-3 and 3-4 depicted the cyclical effect of succeeding generations of increasingly powerful computers. The electronics industry has progressed from vacuum tubes to transistors to integrated semiconductor circuits with ever-increasing densities of circuit packaging. Home entertainment has evolved from the radio to monochrome VHF and UHF television to color television with hundreds of channels via satellite and cable. Most of the businesses with which I have been associated over my career have been technologically driven, so I am particularly sensitive to technological cycles.

In 1983, the consulting firm of Booz Allen and Hamilton proposed an innovative way of looking at life cycles of products that are driven by technology. As shown in Figure 3-7, the Booz Allen view contrasts the level of customer sophistication with the degree of supplier experience. On a plot where supplier experience is the x-axis and customer sophistication the y-axis, the Booz Allen life cycle curve is U-shaped and passes chronologically through four quadrants:[1]

Figure 3-7
Booz Allen Life Cycle Curve

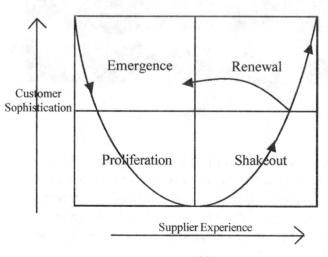

Plan For Profitability!

1) Emergence: The cycle begins in the upper left-hand quadrant with product innovation. In this phase, customers tend to be technologically sophisticated (e.g., early purchasers of personal computers), whereas the cumulative market and production experience of suppliers is nominal.

2) Proliferation: In this stage, the profile of the typical customer shifts from the sophisticated pioneer to that of the mainstream customer with less sophistication. Supplier experience increases and new suppliers enter the market.

3) Shakeout: In the lower right-hand quadrant, the level of customer sophistication begins to increase through exposure to and use of first-generation products. Concurrently, supplier experience concentrates among the market leaders and marginal suppliers drop out of the competition.

4) Renewal: In this quadrant, the Booz Allen life cycle curve takes one of two courses. In most high-technology markets, the curve loops back on itself as the next generation of technology is introduced. The other course is that of the traditional life cycle curve of Figure 3-6, which continues its dead-end course upward and to the right, in which case the surviving competitors concentrate on productivity improvements to maintain their market shares.

---

[1] Harvey L. Poppel, Market-Product Life Cycles-A New Strategic Analysis Tool, 1983, Booz Allen and Hamilton, New York

Lee E. Hargrave, Jr.

STATISTICAL PROJECTION TECHNIQUES

Someone has to bite the bullet and develop a logical forecast of the growth of the SBU's served market over the planning horizon. More often than not, the planner himself does not have to do this himself because forecasts exist in industry literature, i.e., in those secondary sources of market data to which I referred earlier.

In some situations, however, the planner may not be able to uncover any usable forecasts for his served market. In these instances, there are statistical techniques that can be applied to historical market data to derive projections that reflect historical patterns. In fact, these techniques are frequently used by secondary sources to derive their forecasts. It should be emphasized that I am not referring to mere time-series extrapolations of the past into the future, no matter how sophisticated the extrapolative formulas may be.

The approach is to ascertain what factors have shaped the market in the past and to what degree. Once these factors, called *causal variables*, have been identified, the aim is to shift the task from projecting the market itself to projecting the causal variables. Clearly, this approach has merit only if we believe that it will be easier to project the underlying variables than the market itself.

The most useful tool in this regard is that of *multiple linear regression*. If mathematics is not one of your strengths, there is no cause for concern because there are computer programs that perform multiple linear regression. For those of you who are interested in theory, let me digress for a moment and discuss the topic. The rest of you can just skip over this material.

66

Plan For Profitability!

Multiple linear regression attempts to explain the market variable y (the dependent variable) in terms of its causal variables x_i (the independent variables) in the following form:

$$y = c_0 + c_1 x_1 + c_2 x_2 + \ldots + c_n x_n + e$$

The regression is termed *multiple* because there may be more than one causal variable and it is *linear* because each causal variable is assumed to have a linear effect on the dependent variable. In the expression above, c_0 is a constant term and e is the error term, i.e., that amount of behavior of the independent variable that is not explained by the regression equation.

There are several statistics that measure the quality of the regression equation. Foremost among these is *R-squared*, which measures the quality of fit of the regression, i.e., how well the independent causal variables explain the behavior of the dependent market variable. R-squared varies from zero to one; the closer it is to one, the better the quality of the explanation.

Also of importance is the *standard error* of the regression (sigma), which measures the difference between the actual historical values of the dependent variable and those calculated by the regression equation. Sigma may be expressed in percentage terms relative to the mean of the dependent variable. The lower the percentage, the better the regression.

The *elasticities* of each of the independent variables are also important, since they provide an indication of the relative importance among the variables. An elasticity of 0.88 for a given independent variable, for example, denotes that a change of 1.00% in that variable will cause a change of 0.88% in the dependent variable. In short, the higher the elasticity, the more important that variable in determining the value of the independent variable.

Regression techniques have their roots in econometric modeling. When applied to models of served markets, such techniques are generally associated with markets that are sensitive to econometric factors, e.g., inflation, interest rates, disposable income, indices of production, and so forth. Hence, regression techniques are frequently employed to explain and project the behavior of markets that are mature, relatively stable, or both. Examples that come to mind include the markets for automobiles, white goods and machine tools. However, regression modeling can also be applied to extremely dynamic markets, as the following example will illustrate.

In 1984, Storage Technology was attempting to predict its domestic served market for high-capacity magnetic disk drives employed for on-line computer data storage. Although several sources of disk drive market projections were available, the company desired not only to verify these projections, but also to understand better what forces drove its market for disk storage.

Storage Technology was fairly confident that a major determinant was the quantity of high-performance mainframe computer shipments (since the disk drives attach to the computers) and the company was far more comfortable with its projections for computer shipments than for disk drive shipments. Hence, if a cause-and-effect relationship could be uncovered between computer shipments and disk drive shipments, Storage Technology could not only check the projections of its industry sources, but could also generate its own disk drive projections independently of outside sources.

Some industry terms need to be introduced at this point to continue the story. The power of a computer can be measured in terms of the amount of instructions it can execute in a given period of time, which is expressed in millions of instructions per second (mips). Computer storage is measured in eight-bit words (bytes). Storage Technology's challenge was to determine the relationship between shipments of bytes of disk storage (the dependent variable) and shipments of mips of computer power (the independent variable).

Reasonably accurate historical data for byte shipments was available for the years 1978-82, as well as an estimate for 1983. This is displayed as Figure 3-8.

Figure 3-8
Domestic Disk Storage Shipments

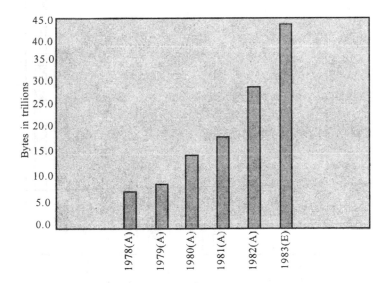

Solid mips data was available back to 1975, as well as a projection through 1987 in which the company had confidence, and these are shown in Figure 3-9.

Through multiple linear regression analysis, the company determined that disk storage shipments in a given year were determined by the computer power shipped in that year *and* in the prior year, along with a small constant term. The simplicity of this conclusion was both appealing and logical. Customers were buying computers with an initial amount of peripheral disk storage and then adding disk drives in the year after purchase as they put all of their applications on line on the computers.

Figure 3-9
Domestic Computer Shipments

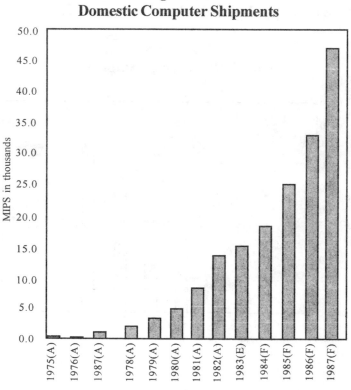

Plan For Profitability!

The resulting fit of the multiple regression was extremely good for such a dynamic industry, with an R-squared of 0.986 and a sigma of 8.4%. The regression equation describing byte shipments (in trillions) as a function of mips shipments (in thousands) was as follows:

$$bytes = 0.006 + 0.8 \times (current\ mips) + 2.68 \times (prior\ mips)$$

The elasticity of mips shipments in the second year was 0.68, versus 0.29 for first-year shipments, which indicated that over two-thirds of the storage associated with computer shipments was shipped in the year *after* the shipments of the computers. With this improved insight into the underlying factors that were driving its disk storage market, Storage Technology was able to project its served market through 1987 with more confidence. This projection is depicted in Figure 3-10.

Figure 3-10
Domestic Disk Storage Shipments

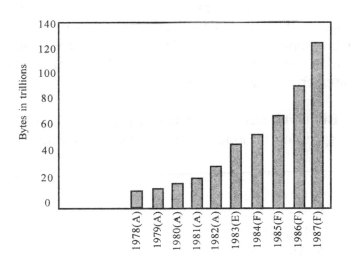

Lee E. Hargrave, Jr.

THE MARKET OF INTERNATIONAL MICROWIDGETS

As mentioned earlier, the market that International Microwidgets serves is the worldwide market for microwidgets. It is a large market, in the neighborhood of $2 billion of shipments annually. Because of its size, the market is followed closely by several market research organizations, among them the Gartner Group, Dataquest and the International Data Group. The result is that there is no shortage of information about the market and its size. By reconciling these diverse sources of data, the company is able to arrive at an historical and forecast quantification of the market in which it has confidence.

International Microwidgets elects to segment its served market into only one dimension, that of geography. The compelling reason for the company's concentration on geographical segmentation is the striking differences among market growth rates throughout the world. For example, the United States market is most mature market in the world, with an AAG of only 10%, while the Asian market is growing at twice that rate, fueled principally by the emerging market in China.

Bill Portes elects to segment the served market of his company into the following six geographical segments:

- United States/Canada
- Latin America
- Western Europe
- Eastern Europe
- Africa/Middle East
- Asia/Pacific

Plan For Profitability!

Because of the dynamic nature of the market for microwidgets, the company's strategic planning horizon is only three years. Its strategic plan contains six years of data, as follows:

- Two years of history: Years -2 and -1, with the annotation (A) for actual
- The current year: Year 0, with the annotation (E) for estimate
- Three year of forecast: Years 1, 2 and 3, with the annotation (F) for forecast

A modest inflation rate of 3.5 % is assumed in the forecast years of the plan. All of the data is presented in current dollars. Figure 3-11 is a tabulation of the served market of International Microwidgets.

Figure 3-11
Worldwide Market for Microwidgets
($ in millions)

Year	-2(A)	-1(A)	0(E)	1(F)	2(F)	3(F)	AAG
U.S./Canada	500	540	600	660	720	800	10%
Latin America	100	120	140	160	180	200	15%
Western Europe	440	480	540	600	680	760	12%
Eastern Europe	120	160	180	220	260	300	20%
Africa/ Middle East	80	80	100	120	120	140	12%
Asia/ Pacific	300	360	440	520	640	760	20%
Total	1540	1740	2000	2280	2600	2960	14%

Figure 3-12 is the same data presented in graphical form.

Figure 3-12
Worldwide Market for Microwidgets

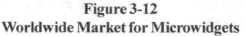

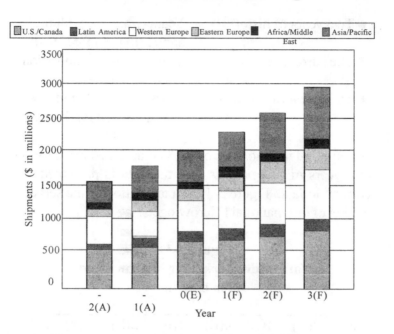

SUMMARY

Of the several points made in this chapter about the market, I hope that you will remember at least the following:

• An SBU must be able to define the market it serves in clear and unambiguous terms.

• It will probably be informative to segment the market along one or more dimensions to provide insight into its composition. However, the data collection process can become prohibitive if segmentation is overdone.

- Strategic planners seldom perform primary market research. Rather, they rely upon secondary sources of data, which are usually adequate.

- Markets may be quantified in units, dollars or both. The use of current dollars is preferable to constant dollars.

- Market growth rate is the single most important measure of the attractiveness of a market. Accuracy is not particularly important.

- It is important to understand what underlying factors drive the behavior of the market. The recognition of market trends and cycles form part of this understanding. Statistical projection techniques, notably multiple linear regression, can also be valuable tools.

Now comes the work. The first step is to decide whether to quantify your company's served market in units, dollars or both. The next step is to decide whether it is instructive to segment the market, keeping in mind that every dimension of segmentation increases the amount of data that has to be generated and manipulated. Finally, the market must be quantified, both historically and over the planning horizon. Whatever means you employ to project the served market (secondary sources, primary sources or statistical projection techniques), keep in mind that the credibility of the strategic plan rests squarely on the credibility of your market projections. Good luck!

CHAPTER IV

COMPETITION

A horse never runs so fast as when he has other horses to catch up and outpace.

Ovid, circa A.D. 8

The price which society pays for the law of competition, like the price it pays for cheap comforts and luxuries, is great; but the advantages of this law are also greater still than its cost.

Andrew Carnegie, 1889

So long as some are strong and some are weak, the weak will be driven to the wall.

W. Somerset Maugham, 1938

The market and competition sections of the strategic plan form an entity that is referred to as the *uncontrollable environment*, that portion of the SBU's environment over which it has little to no control. To be sure, there are some exceptions to this notion, such as the situations of innovators that create markets that did not previously exist and, in effect, control them during the early periods of their growth. Examples that come to mind include Ford's creation and early dominance of the domestic market for mass-produced automobiles, the early lead by Univac in computers and Dumont Laboratories pioneering work in television. In a free-market economy, however, there inevitably emerges competition over which the market innovator has no control. To wit, Ford is now one of many players in the worldwide automobile market, and as for Univac and Dumont, they no longer exist as identifiable businesses.

In all of these instances, competitors emerged and implemented strategies that were effective in eating into the shares of the market leaders and eventually dethroning them. In the case of Univac, for example, IBM chose not to compete head-to-head against Univac's superior technological strength, but outflanked Univac by shifting the battle from technology to marketing, an arena in which IBM was a seasoned veteran and Univac a neophyte. Ironically, IBM was later challenged on the technological front in personal computers by such companies as Microsoft and Intel.

The objective of the competition section of the strategic plan is to understand the competitors well enough to develop strategies for the SBU that defend against the competitors' strengths and attack their weaknesses. It is helpful to view this exercise as consisting of three elements:

- The development of objective listings of the strengths and weaknesses of each of the SBU's principal competitors. Strengths and weaknesses should be referenced to the norms of the market, not to the SBU's own competitive posture.

- Synthesis of the strategies that the competitors are expected to follow over the time span of the strategic plan. These strategies should correlate with the competitors' strengths and weaknesses and with their current strategies.

- Ultimately, articulating the opportunities and threats that the competitive scenario presents to the SBU. This must be done in the context of the *total* environment, i.e., the market, the competition and the SBU's own situation. This step is covered in Chapter V.

MARKET SHARE

Just as market growth is the most important absolute measure of the served market, market share is the most important measure of each competitor's positioning within the served market. Superficially, market share is a simple concept: a company's volume in the served market divided by the total volume in the market, expressed either in unit terms or in dollar terms. This simplicity can be deceptive, however, as the following example will illustrate.

Consider the market described in Figure 4-1, in which there are only four competitors: the SBU and companies A, B and C. According to the SBU, the served market consists of 1000 unit shipments annually and the SBU contends that it has a 30% share of the market. The SBU's share data shows that company A is the leading competitor with 40% of the market, while companies B and C have shares of 20% and 10%, respectively.

Figure 4-1
SBU's Served Market

	Annual Shipments	Market Share
Company A	400	40 %
SBU	300	30
Company B	200	20
Company C	100	10
Total	1000	100 %

However, an interview with the director of marketing at company C reveals an entirely different set of market statistics. According to company C, it is the leading competitor in its served market with a share of 50%. The SBU is in second place with 30% of the market, company B has the remaining 20%, and company A is not even viewed as a competitor in company C's market.

Which set of data is correct? Both are. Remember that the denominator of market share is the served market and that the market that a company serves is defined *by that company*. The message is that no two companies, even arch competitors, are likely to define their served markets in precisely the same way.

In this instance, company C has a much narrower view of its served market than does the SBU, as is shown in Figure 4-2. Due either to a narrower product line or to less customer access than the SBU, company C reckons that its served market is only 200 units per year, with these units apportioned among the competitors as shown in Figure 4-2.

Figure 4-2
Company C's Served Market

	Annual Shipments	Market Share
Company C	100	50 %
SBU	60	30
Company B	40	20
Total	200	100 %

Figure 4-3 depicts the four companies' views of their served markets in the form of a Venn diagram. In this example, the SBU and company B have identical definitions of the served market (notwithstanding the prior comment that this situation is unlikely). Company C's market is a subset of the SBU's. Company A serves a far larger market than the SBU, but does not serve any of company C's market.

Let me complicate this example even more. It turns out in this example that we also have access to the director of strategic planning at company B, who disputes the SBU's market share figures as documented in Figure 4-1, despite the fact that company B and the SBU agree upon the scope of the served market. Company B claims that it is the market leader with a 40% share, and that the SBU, company A and company C follow with shares of 30%, 20% and 10%, respectively.

How can this be? Again, company B's view of the market is valid and perfectly legitimate from its perspective. Company B concentrates on products at the upper end of the pricing spectrum relative to its competition. From the table of Figure 4-4, company B's products are priced in the Cadillac range of $200 per unit ($40,000 divided by 200 units), whereas the average price of the products of the SBU and of company C is $100 per unit, and company A averages only $50 per unit. Company B feels that its share of the *dollar* market is more representative of its penetration and it is difficult to refute this point of view.

Figure 4-3
The Companies' Views of Their Served Markets

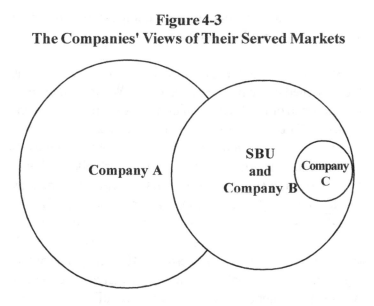

Figure 4-4
Company B's Served Market

	Annual Shipments in Units	Average Price per Unit	Annual Shipments in Dollars	Market Share
Company B	200	$200	$40,000	40%
SBU	300	100	30,000	30
Company A	400	50	20,000	20
Company C	100	100	10,000	10
Total	1000		$100,000	100%

There are two points that I am trying to make. First, since it is our strategic plan, it is our definition of the served market that governs the plan. Second, be prepared for the possibility of conflicting data about market size and share from other sources, since competitors may define the market differently than we do.

Seldom is the number of competitors in a market as few as the four cited in the foregoing example. When markets narrow down to only a handful of competitors, it is usually indicative of the competitive shakeout that accompanies markets in the stage of maturity or decline. Witness the consolidations and shakeout in the domestic automobile market in the 1950's and the demise of such legendary names as Studebaker, Hudson, LaSalle, Nash and DeSoto. By the mid-1950's, only four competitors were left in the market: General Motors, Ford, Chrysler and American Motors, with the latter hanging on by its fingernails. The emergence of foreign competition, notably the Japanese, altered the competitive scenario later on, of course, but one could view the foreign competitors
as introducing a new generation to the market and, in effect, looping around the Booz Allen life cycle curve of Figure 3-7.

It is not uncommon to encounter markets in which there are two or three dozen viable competitors. I performed an analysis of the emerging market for word processors in 1980 and identified 35 competitors in the United States and Canada alone. Clearly, it is impractical to analyze in detail such a large number of companies. As a general rule, I prefer to restrict my competitive analysis to the top five companies in the market or to those with market shares of 10% or greater.

CHRONOLOGICAL MARKET SHARE DATA

Of course, the market share analysis should not be confined to a single year as suggested by the examples of

Figure 4-1 through 4-4, but should cover the entire historical frame of reference of the strategic plan. For an example of the format that I prefer to portray historical market share data, see Figures 4-5 through 4-7, which show the market growth and share distribution for oil well pumping units. In these examples, the historical retrospective is five years, the market is quantified in terms of units (versus dollars), and the analysis is confined to the top four competitors in the market.

SOURCES OF COMPETITIVE DATA

To the layman, the term *competitive intelligence* conjures up images of industrial espionage, wiretaps, listening devices, payoffs to competitors' employees to obtain proprietary information, and the much publicized legal proceedings of those who are caught. Although it would be naive to deny that such unethical activity does exist, it is surely insignificant in comparison with the legal and ethical intelligence activities conducted by modern companies.

Early in my career, I spent several years in the field of military intelligence. It is not generally appreciated that sources of military intelligence are usually mundane and in the public domain and are seldom as sensational as those cited in the preceding paragraph. So also is the case with business intelligence.

Figure 4-5
Worldwide Market for Oil-Well Pumping Units

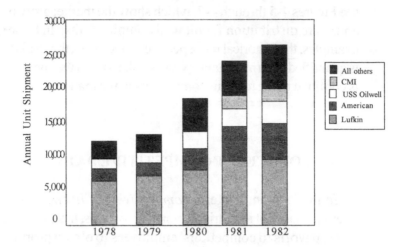

Figure 4-6
Worldwide Market Growth
for Oil-Well Pumping Units
(Annual Unit Shipments)

	1978	1979	1980	1981	1982	AAG
Lufkin	5,700	6,500	8,000	9,600	10,000	15%
American	2,100	2,300	3,200	4,500	4,600	22%
USS Oilwell	1,300	1,400	2,000	2,700	2,800	21%
CMI				1,600	1,700	NA
All others	2,400	2,700	4,500	5,400	6,900	30%
Total Market	11,500	12,900	17,700	23,800	26,000	23%

Plan For Profitability!

Figure 4-7
Worldwide Market Shares
for Oil-Well Pumping Units
(Annual Unit Shipments)

	1978	1979	1980	1981	1982
Lufkin	50%	50%	45%	40%	38%
American	18	18	18	19	18
USS Oilwell	11	11	11	11	11
CMI	0	0	0	7	7
All others	21	21	26	23	26
Total Market	100%	100%	100%	100%	100%

Any company that intends to become or remain a competitive force in its served markets must maintain current dossiers on all of its major competitors. There is often a specific individual or group within the marketing organization that is charged with this responsibility. I have seen situations where the competitive analysis group had so finely honed its skills that it could recognize telegraphic signals from key competitors and predict their actions in the market with admirable accuracy.

At the top of the list of sources of competitive intelligence are the SBU's own *customers*. They are the single most common point of contact between the SBU and its competitors. Competitors are motivated to discuss their forward plans with customers to promote products and capture business, and customers are likewise motivated to discuss these plans with other competitors to stimulate competition and avail themselves of a wider range of choices, better products and services, lower prices or all of the above. It is important to recognize that this is a two-way street; just as an SBU taps its customers for information about the competition, so also are the competitors doing the same thing.

Second on my list of sources of competitive intelligence is that *literature* of the competitors that is available to the public. Included in this category are annual reports, quarterly reports, reports of shareholders' meetings, press releases, product catalogs and brochures, price lists, trade advertising and patents. It is interesting to note that the responsibility for preparing the foregoing literature is generally dispersed within any company; i.e., no single individual within the company is familiar with the contents of the entire spectrum of the company's literature. This observation leads me to the bizarre speculation that the most knowledgeable individuals on the contents of a company's public literature may reside not in the company, but in the competitive analysis groups of the company's competitors.

Third-party sources also rank high on any checklist. These include trade journals, product survey and comparison literature, the proceedings of business symposia, market research publications, and all the like literature that passes across any individual's desk after he or she has been immersed in an industry for a sufficient period of time.

Also, do not rule out *direct contact* with the competition. Of course, such contact must preclude any suggestion of collusion or other impropriety, but it can turn out to be the most efficient method of obtaining some information. When I attend trade shows, for example, I always make a point of visiting the exhibits of my company's competitors. My approach is straightforward, even sometimes disarming. I introduce myself and my affiliation without obfuscation and explain that I want to understand why a customer would prefer the competitor's products to those of my company. If nothing else, I gather a portfolio of points with which to play the devil's advocate in strategy sessions back on my home turf.

Another perfectly legal source of competitive insight is to *purchase competitive products* and evaluate them, including tearing them down to understand how they function. Some companies take this strategy a step further and copy or improve upon the designs. Much of the success of Japanese companies in world markets has its roots in deliberately copying and improving European and American products in the 1950's and 1960's.

COMPETITORS' STRENGTHS AND WEAKNESSES

Ultimately, all of the market share data and associated competitive intelligence must be distilled into a concise articulation of the strengths and weaknesses of each significant competitor within the SBU's served market. As mentioned earlier, my preference is to restrict the number of competitors under evaluation to a single-digit number. Likewise, I prefer to restrict the number of both strengths and weaknesses of each competitor to a comparable number. It is easier to view the entire panorama of all of the competitors' strengths and weaknesses if it consists of a restricted number of judiciously selected facts. The mere process of sorting the facts down to a manageable number forces the analyst to decide what is important and what is not.

The process of articulating competitors' strengths and weaknesses has become so ingrained in my thought processes that it is second nature and challenging for me to describe. Upon reflection, though, I suppose that I have a mental checklist that contains at least the following elements:

- **Market Share:** What is the competitor's current market share? Has it been increasing, decreasing or stable? In what particular segments of the market is the competitor particularly strong or weak?

- **Image:** How is the competitor perceived in the market by the customer? Is this image warranted or outdated?

- **Product:** How do the competitor's product offerings compare versus other products in the market? Specifically, how do the products rate in terms of performance, features, innovation, reliability, serviceability, cost of manufacture, proprietary protection, etc.?

- **Marketing:** How does the competitor's method of distribution compare with other companies in the served market? What are the breadth, depth and quality of its sales coverage? How effective is its advertising? On balance, is the competitor's marketing effort an asset or a liability?

- **Engineering:** Is the competitor noted for a strong, innovative engineering team? Are there any deficiencies in the skill mix? Does the company perform its own research and development?

Plan For Profitability!

- Manufacturing: To what degree is the competitor vertically integrated? What is the split between internal manufacturing and external purchases? How modern are the manufacturing facilities? Where are they geographically situated relative to major markets? What are their capacities? What is the competitor's intrinsic cost of production?

- Finance: What are the competitor's product margins and overall profitability? Are inventory, payables and receivables within acceptable norms? Does the competitor have adequate capacity for debt and access to capital? Is the company a user or a generator of cash?

- Management: What are the experience, credibility and dedication of the management team? Are there any glaring weaknesses?

LISTING STRENGTHS AND WEAKNESSES

At the close of Chapter II, I made reference to the case study of the Head Ski Company[1]. This case has survived some 30 years of analysis in business schools and is still a staple of the literature, which truly attests to the relevancy of the lessons it contains. I must also confess that, as an avid skier, I can relate to the case. The Head Ski case traces the story of Howard Head, the inventor and pioneer of the world's first production metal ski, from the early 1950's to the mid-1960's, at which time the Head Ski Company was the recognized leader in the worldwide ski market.

---

[1] C. Roland Christensen et al, op cit

Let us place ourselves for a moment in the role of a competitor of the Head Ski Company in the mid-1960's, when Head had reached its zenith in the market. How would we have assessed the strengths and weaknesses of the Head Ski Company? Recognizing my personal bias toward simplicity, I would have distilled the list down to four strengths and three weaknesses, presenting them in a single table so that the essence of the Head Ski Company as a competitor could be absorbed in a single scan. The following is my assessment of Head as a competitor in the mid-1960's:

Strengths

- The leading share of the worldwide ski market, with particular strength at the high-priced end of the market.

- An image as the status ski on the market, which is enhanced by Head's recognized leadership in metal ski technology and its distinctive all-black decor.

- A select and loyal network of distributors, all of which can easily market other sports equipment and sportswear.

- A strong balance sheet, high profitability and a very high price-to-earnings multiple (50x) on its shares.

Weaknesses

- One-man management, with little depth or breadth beyond Howard Head.

- Little R&D in non-metal (fiberglass) skis and lack of recognition that such materials could pose a threat to metal skis.

- Sparse distribution coverage of the European market.

Let me stress that there are no standards of absolute correctness in the above exercise. Many of my business school students developed presentations of Head Ski's strengths and weaknesses that were as good (well, almost as good) as my example. The point is that all such well conceived lists for the Head case have common themes among them, viz., market share, image, distribution and financial strengths, and weaknesses in management, reaction to the fiberglass threat and European marketing. The first and crucial step in competitive analysis is that the competitors' strengths and weaknesses be recognized, articulated and agreed upon by all concerned.

COMPETITORS' STRATEGIES

The second step is to attempt to synthesize the strategy that each competitor is likely to follow over the time span of the strategic plan. This entails documenting the competitor's observed prior strategy and factoring in competitive intelligence to induce its strategy in the future. In most instances, past, current and future strategies will not be dissimilar. Companies, like people, are very slow to change their ways.

Synthesis of competitors' strategies is an exercise in inductive reasoning (see Chapter I) at its purest and is one of the steps in the planning process that I enjoy the most. My approach is to close the door to my office, switch my tele phone to voicemail, post the competitors' strengths and weaknesses on the wall where they can be seen easily, put my feet up on the desk, and ask myself the question, "If I had these strengths and weaknesses, what would I do?"

This question presupposes that (a) you are rational and (b) your competitor is as rational as you are, which is consistent with the maxim of not underestimating the competition. In fact, at times the competitor will be smarter than you, if only because it has more facts at its disposal about its situation than you do.

THE STRATEGY SUMMARY

Let me continue with the example of the Head Ski Company as we make the transition from assessment of a competitor's strengths and weaknesses to the synthesis of its strategy. You should recognize, however, that this is an easy example, for we have the advantage of knowing what Head's strategy was in the late 1960's and the early 1970's merely by researching the business literature. Nevertheless, since we have come this far, let me continue.

In light of the list of four strengths and three weaknesses, the Head Ski Company could rationally be expected to pursue most, if not all, of the following elements of strategy:

- Leverage its image of quality and its leading share position in the high-priced segment of the market to introduce a line of medium-priced metal skis to capture that growing segment of the market.

92

Plan For Profitability!

- Capitalize upon its strong network of distributors and its reputation for quality products by expanding into other ski equipment and into premium skiwear.

- Search for synergistic acquisitions, with priority to companies with strengths in fiberglass skis or European distribution, using the company's high-multiple stock in lieu of cash to finance the acquisitions.

- In any event, intensify efforts in fiberglass research and development.

- Bring in professional manufacturing, marketing and financial management to complement the founder's talents.

As it turned out, the Head Ski Company followed only a fraction of the hypothesized strategy, which made it easier for its competitors to topple it from its position of leadership. The company did expand into skiwear and establish an image and position in high-priced skiwear comparable to that of its metal ski line. Management changes were made, but the company still bore the stamp of its entrepreneurial founder and the attendant weaknesses. The company continued to lag in the development of fiberglass skis, which eventually displaced all forms of wooden and metal skis from the market. And in contrast to being an acquirer, the financial health of Head Ski declined, and the company was subsequently acquired by AMF.

Lee E. Hargrave, Jr.

THE COMPETITORS OF INTERNATIONAL
MICROWIDGETS

International Microwidgets can identify 12 suppliers of
microwidgets to the worldwide market. Several of these,
however, serve niche markets by concentrating on specific
industries, applications or geographic areas. The market
shares of these niche suppliers are small and in decline. At
the other extreme, the top four suppliers in the market collectively command a 90% share. For this reason, the company's
strategic plan focuses on these four companies.

As previously mentioned, the leading company in the market is International Microwidgets itself. The company's share
of the worldwide market is approximately 40 %. Of the six
geographical areas into which the worldwide market has been
segmented, International Microwidgets is the leading competitor in two of the areas: United States/Canada and Latin
America. The company believes that it is the second leading
supplier in three areas: Western Europe, Eastern Europe and
Asia/Pacific. In the sixth area, Africa/Middle East, the company believes that it the third largest supplier.

Headquartered in Tokyo, the second leading competitor is
Microwidgets Ichiban, with a worldwide market share that is
estimated by International Microwidgets to be in the neighborhood of 25%. Ichiban is clearly the leading supplier in its
home market area, Asia/Pacific, and is the second largest
competitor in the United States/Canada.

A German company, Deutsche Microwidgets GmbH, is in
third place on a worldwide basis with a market share

estimated at 20%. Headquartered in Munich, Deutsche is the leading company in its home market, as well as in the Eastern Europe and Africa/Middle East areas.

The fourth competitor is General Widgets, which we discussed in the first chapter. Now, over 25 years since the company declined to act on Bill Portes's concept of incorporating microelectronics in the widget, General Widgets is a shadow of its former greatness. Its worldwide market share has shrunk to a mere 5%, which is concentrated in certain niche markets in the United States/Canada and Latin America. The company's profitability has suffered in recent years and the health of its balance sheet has deteriorated.

International Microwidgets also tracks eight other competitors, none of which have worldwide market shares in excess of 2%. These competitors are based in France, Italy, the Netherlands, the United Kingdom, South Korea, Taiwan, Canada and the United States.

Figure 4-8 displays the best estimates of International Microwidgets of the worldwide revenues of the leading competitors for the past two years and for the present year. Figure 4-9 is simply the same data converted into market share.

Figure 4-8
Worldwide Market for Microwidgets
($ in millions)

Year	-2(A)	-1(A)	0(E)	AAG
International Microwidgets	580	680	800	17%
Microwidgets Ichiban	360	420	500	18%
Deutsche Microwidgets	285	330	400	18%
General Widgets	115	110	100	-7%
Others	200	200	200	0%
Total	1540	1740	2000	14%

Figure 4-9
Shares of the Worldwide Market for Microwidgets

Year	-2(A)	-1(A)	0(E)
International Microwidgets	38%	39%	40%
Microwidgets Ichiban	23%	24%	25%
Deutsche Microwidgets	19%	19%	20%
General Widgets	7%	6%	5%
Others	13%	12%	10%
Total	100%	100%	100%

International Microwidgets has also estimated its competitors' positioning in the six geographical areas into which it segments the world market. Space precludes me from showing the historical data, but Figure 4-10 shows the company's best assessment of the competitive scenario in the six areas in the current year.

Figure 4-10
Worldwide Microwidget Market by Area
Current Year
($ in millions)

	U.S./Canada	L.America	W.Europe	E.Europe	Africa/M.E.	Asia/Pacific	Total
Int'l Micro.	400	90	160	40	20	90	800
Ichiban	170	20	50	10	30	220	500
Deutsche	20	10	230	80	50	10	400
General	80	20	--	--	--	--	100
Others	30	--	80	10	--	80	200
Total	700	140	520	140	100	400	2000

As you can see from Figure 4-10, International Microwidgets is the leader in the United States/Canada and the Latin America areas, Ichiban dominates the market in the Asia/Pacific region, and Deutsche Microwidgets is the leader in the other three areas.

Microwidgets Ichiban

Microwidgets Ichiban was founded in the late 1970's as a venture of one of Japan's leading semiconductor companies. Ichiban's entry into microwidgets was via *reverse engineering*. The company painstakingly disassembled several microwidgets that it had purchased from Bill Portes's company, analyzed the principles of operation of the device, and copied the design employing Japanese microchips with sufficient distinctions such that the Japanese design did not infringe upon any of the proprietary features of the International Microwidgets product. Since then, Ichiban has added significant improvements to the original design so that its image as a cloner has been supplanted by that of an innovator.

With its captive source of microchips, Ichiban has the potential to be the lowest cost manufacturer in the market. Its manufacturing costs have gradually been reduced in recent years to the point where they are approaching those of the market leader, International Microwidgets. As Ichiban accumulates more volume, it is only a matter of time until its costs better those of its American competitor.

Ichiban is the largest competitor of International Microwidgets in its home market, United States/Canada, where Ichiban have been accused (but never formally incriminated) of dumping to acquire market share. Of more concern to Portes, however, is Ichiban's dominating presence in the Asia/Pacific market. This market is projected to grow at 20% per year over the planning horizon, which, along with Eastern Europe, represents the fastest growth of the six geographic areas. Most of this growth is anticipated to be derived from markets outside Japan, with a large portion of it coming from China.

With this background in mind, Bill Portes's concise evaluation of the strengths, weaknesses and probable strategies of Microwidgets Ichiban is as follows:

Strengths

- Low cost of manufacture, with a captive source of semiconductor components

- Image as an innovator

- Leading market share in the Asia/Pacific region (55%)

Plan For Profitability!

- Second leading market share in the United States/Canada region (24%)

Weaknesses

- Less significant market share in the other four re- gions of the world (12%)

- Exports into major markets hampered by Japan's trade surpluses and the strong yen

Probable Strategies

- Focus top priority on dominating the emerging markets in the Asia/Pacific region

- Continue to drive down manufacturing costs with accumulated volume coupled with value engineering

- Compete in the other markets of the world by reducing profit margins where feasible

Deutsche Microwidgets

Deutsche Microwidgets GmbH was founded at about the same time as International Microwidgets. Unlike Microwidgets Ichiban, however, Deutsche pursued an original design for its product line, which has a distinctly European appearance. Among the three leaders in worldwide market share, Deutsche is undeniably the highest-cost manufacturer because of high labor rates at its manufacturing facilities in Munich and higher costs for micro-)

chips from its European semiconductor suppliers.

Under the umbrella of the European Community, Deutsche Microwidgets is the leader in the Western Europe region with an estimated share of 44% of the market. Bill Portes has been pleased with his company's performance in the region, where it ranks second with a 31% market share. Of more concern to him is the German presence in the expanding market of Eastern Europe, which, while smaller than the Asia/Pacific region, is forecast to grow as rapidly at 20% per year. Portes captures the profile of Deutsche Microwidgets as follows:

<u>Strengths</u>

- Image as a quality product

- Leading market share in the Western Europe region (44%)

- Leading market share in the rapidly growing Eastern Europe region (57%) and in the Africa/Middle East region (50%)

<u>Weaknesses</u>

- High selling prices due to high cost of manufacture

- Negligible presence in the United States/Canada and Asia/Pacific regions (3%)

Plan For Profitability!

<u>Probable Strategies</u>

- Concentrate exports on those regions of traditional strength for European companies: Eastern Europe and Africa/Middle East

- Pursue other regions opportunistically by promoting the superior quality of the product line

- Reduce manufacturing costs as feasible through increased volumes

General Widgets

Oh, how the mighty have fallen! To think that just 25 years ago General Widgets ruled world of widgets and had the keys to continued supremacy in its grasp. Unfortunately, the company was woefully late to recognize the widget revolution. Some five years after Bill Portes left General Widgets, the company finally woke up and mounted an impressive effort to convert its product line to electronics. Despite investing over half of its net worth in the project to catch up, General Widgets was never able to do so.

Today, the company's annual revenues have shrunk to $100 million. Despite extensive cost-cutting efforts, the company has lost money in three of the past five years. Its share of the United States/Canada market has dwindled to 11% and most of these customers would have already converted to other suppliers were it not for the cost of conversion.

The dismal situation at General Widgets actually portends a major opportunity for Bill Portes and International Microwidgets, but it will take us two more chapters to discuss the opportunity and the ensuing strategy, and not until the penultimate chapter in the book will we be equipped to implement the strategy. For the time being, please be content with this brief assessment by Portes of the state of his former employer:

Strength

- A substantial customer base in the United States/Canada and Latin America regions

Weakness

- Precarious financial position

Probable Strategies

- Continue to look for a rescuer

- Failing that, consider protection under the bankruptcy laws

SUMMARY

Understanding the competition is vital to the creation of a realistic strategic plan. Among the important aspects of competitive analysis are the following:

- Market share is the single most important measure of a competitor's position. Share should always be referenced to the SBU's served market.

Plan For Profitability!

- Competitive intelligence is a perfectly legal and accepted function in most companies, particularly the more successful ones. Sources of competitive intelligence include customers, the open literature, third parties, direct contact and competitors' actual products.

- If the SBU has numerous competitors in its served market, it should focus on a manageable number of them, e.g., the top five or those with shares above 10%.

- It is imperative that consensus be reached within the SBU on the strengths and weaknesses of each of the key competitors, since these form the foundation for subsequent elements of the strategic plan.

- Factors to consider in developing strengths and weaknesses are market share, image, product, marketing, engineering, manufacturing, finance and management.

- In synthesizing a competitor's anticipated strategy, the SBU should never underestimate its foe. If the competitor pursues a less aggressive course of action, then the SBU is even more well prepared.

Now you have to get to work again. Your first step is to identify the key competitors in your company's served market. Try to keep the list short so that you can focus on the important players in the market. Keeping the list short will also keep the amount of work that has to be done in this section within reasonable bounds.

Then, for each competitor, attempt to quantify that competitor's historical share of the served market. Do not attempt to project the competitor's share of the market over the planning horizon. You simply do not have enough information at this stage in the development of your plan to do so.

At this point in the preparation of the strategic plan, I usually have to make the first iteration of previously generated information. Market data is usually derived from several sources and, more often than not, there are disagreements among them. It is likely that you encountered some conflicting data when you quantified the served market at the end of the last chapter, but you probably reconciled the differences to arrive at a market quantification that you felt comfortable with.

Now, however, you may have competitive market share data that presents even more conflicts. Perhaps the sum of the most liberal market share estimates amounts to more than 100% of the market or, to the other extreme, the sum of the most conservative estimates falls well short of 100%. You may decide to go back and adjust the size of the served market as part of the reconciliation of this conflicting data. The positive side to this exercise is that each new piece of information improves your understanding of the market and strengthens confidence in your estimates of the served market and the leading competitors' shares.

Next, attempt to articulate each competitor's strengths and weaknesses, using the checklist of market share, image, product, marketing, engineering, manufacturing, finance and management. Again, try to keep each list brief and concise.

Finally, for each competitor, ask yourself the question, "If I had this market share and these strengths and weaknesses, what would be my strategy?" Then, write it down.

To remind you, do not strive for perfection at this point. Just as the served market data that you generated in the last chapter may have been modified as a result of your better understanding of competitors' shares, so also may this competitive section be improved by better understanding later in the preparation of the plan.

CHAPTER V

CONSOLIDATING THE ENVIRONMENT

Know thyself.
   Inscription on the Oracle of Apollo at Delphi, Greece (6th
                                                     century B.C.)

People think that at the top there isn't much room. They tend
to think of it as an Everest. My message is that there is tons of
room at the top.
                                           Margaret Thatcher, 1988

When written in Chinese the word crisis is composed of two
characters. One represents danger and the other represents
opportunity.
                                             John F. Kennedy, 1959

The third and final element of the strategic environment is
the SBU itself. Whereas the market and the competitive environment are essentially outside the control of the SBU, its
own situation should be largely within its sphere of control.
For this reason, the SBU's situation is referred to as the *controllable environment*.

Figure 5-1 summarizes the principal elements of the environment in flow-chart form. What we are attempting to arrive at as a result of the investigation into the business environment is an incisive understanding of those *opportunities*
and *threats* that confront the SBU currently or are likely to
confront the SBU at some time over the planning horizon.
Opportunities and threats may be generated by one or more
of three sources:

Plan For Profitability!

- The market environment, where opportunities and threats take the form of favorable or unfavorable trends in the SBU's served market. The rate of market growth (AAG) is an important quantifier in describing the served market.

- The competitive environment, where the strengths and weaknesses of the SBU's major competitors give rise to strategies with which the SBU must contend. Market share is an important measure in quantifying the potency of the competition.

- Within the SBU, where opportunities and threats are likely to be spawned by the inherent strengths and weaknesses of the SBU itself.

Figure 5-1
The Environmental Consolidation

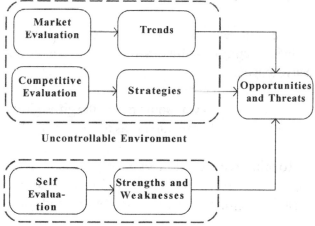

SBU STRENGTHS AND WEAKNESSES

In the last chapter, we covered in some detail the process by which a competitor's strengths and weaknesses could be developed and classified so as to highlight the salient assets and liabilities that each competitor brings to the market arena. The checklist of topical considerations included market share, image, product, marketing, engineering, manufacturing, finance and management. In theory, when an SBU analyzes its own strengths and weaknesses, the process is exactly the same as with its competitors.

In practice, however, there is a major challenge in the SBU's self-evaluation that is not present when the SBU analyzes its competitors. The challenge is to be *objective*. I have yet to encounter a company that could objectively assess its own strengths and weaknesses. The tendency is to exaggerate the strengths and downplay (or even ignore) the weaknesses. Were the situation otherwise, I venture that there would be far fewer management consultants in business than there are.

The 18th-century Scottish poet, Robert Burns, summed up the difficulty of self-assessment in two classic lines in his native tongue:

"O wad some power the giftie gie us
To see oursels as others see us."[1]

To reinforce the point, let us play a role game for a moment. Assume the role of Howard Head, the founder of the Head Ski Company. It is the mid-1960's, and you have

---

[1] Roberts Burns, To a Louse

single-handedly built your company from scratch to the leading ski company in the world and one of the success stories of American industry. You are asked to assess the strengths and weaknesses of Head Ski at that point in time.

How likely is it that you would arrive at a listing comparable to that which one of your competitors derived in the last chapter? Those strengths and weaknesses follow in condensed form:

Strengths

- Leading market share, especially at the high end

- Image as the status ski

- Excellent domestic distribution

- Solid financial position

Weaknesses

- One-man management

- Insufficient R&D in fiberglass skis

- Incomplete European market coverage

Now the sensitivity of the situation becomes apparent. As the founder of the company, you would undoubtedly bridle at the suggestion that the management approach that brought the company to its current pinnacle of success had any deficiencies whatsoever. Although you might acknowledge the potential of fiberglass skis, you would point to the extensive research and development that your company is continuing to sink into improving the metal ski and the expectation that metal skis will command a major share of the market for years to come.

Perhaps now the point about objectivity in the process of self-evaluation has been made. In retrospect, if the Head Ski Company had developed a strategy that addressed the above strengths and weaknesses (with particular emphasis on early entry into fiberglass skis), the Head Ski case would not be the classic of business literature that it is.

In the mid-1970's, Storage Technology Corporation was a company with six years of operating history and annual revenues in the regime of $100 million. The company had developed a line of high-performance tape drives for data storage applications and was beginning to challenge IBM in this small segment of the data processing market. A strategic assessment of Storage Technology at that time (resurrected from the company's archives and edited by the author) reveals that the company had the following view of its own strengths and weaknesses:

Strengths

- The reputation for technologically superior products, competitive prices and responsive service

- Number two in market share (behind IBM) in the tape drive market, with rapid growth in the number of customer installations

Plan For Profitability!

- An aggressive, highly competent, entrepreneurial management team

Weaknesses

- A limited product offering in the context of the total data processing product spectrum

- Negligible market penetration outside the United States

Relative to the foregoing self-assessment of its own strengths and weaknesses, Storage Technology's strategy for the ensuing ten years was directed toward diminishing its weaknesses while simultaneously preserving its strengths. From its initial offering of tape drives, the company expanded in a deliberate manner into magnetic disk storage (1975), printers (by acquisition in 1980) and optical disk storage (1984). Concurrently, the company began to establish its presence outside the United States, with the result that, ten years later, it had wholly owned subsidiaries in all of the developed countries of the free world, and international revenues constituted one-quarter of total corporate revenues.

But even Storage Technology's self-assessment was flawed, particularly in its assessment of its own managerial strengths. Like so many companies that experience rapid growth, Storage Technology failed to assess whether its "aggressive, highly competent, entrepreneurial management team," a perceived strength at $100 million in revenues, would be viewed in the same light at revenues of several times that amount. In the seven-year span from 1975 to 1982, revenues increased tenfold to in excess of $1 billion annually, but profit margins failed to keep pace, such that by 1983, the company was losing money.

In 1981, exuding confidence from its previous successful entries into disk storage and printers, Storage Technology decided to enter the capital-intensive mainframe computer market, only to be forced to withdraw three years later (before it had shipped a single computer) to stem the flow of red ink. Losses continued through 1984 and in the fourth quarter of that year Storage Technology filed for Chapter XI protection. Although there were several root causes to Storage Technology's misfortunes, one of them was clearly that the entrepreneurial team that built the company did not have the background and foresight to install the requisite operational controls for a $1 billion company.

DETERMINING OPPORTUNITIES AND THREATS

At this point in the development of the strategic plan, all of the foregoing environmental analyses of Chapters III, IV and V come together in the form of those *opportunities* and *threats* that confront the SBU or are likely to confront the SBU over the period of the plan. If you have been engrossed in the preparation of your strategic plan to this point in the process, the salient opportunities and threats should figuratively leap out of your pile of working papers and demand to be articulated. If this is not the case, a modest degree of rigor can be brought to the process.

Opportunities and threats arise as a result of favorable or unfavorable interactions between the controllable and the uncontrollable environment. This is, in my opinion, a mechanistic way of explaining what should be common sense, but it may help to cement the concept. Recall from Figure 5-1 that the controllable environment consists of the SBU's own situation, while the uncontrollable environment is described in terms of market trends and competitors' strategies. The interactions to which we should be attuned may be described in process form as follows:

Controllable
Environment
    plus   }   Opportunities and Threats
Uncontrollable
Environment

More specifically, the interactions are:

 SBU Strengths
and Weaknesses
    plus   }   Opportunities and Threats
Market Trends or
Competitors' Strategies

Relative to the SBU, market trends may be described as favorable, unfavorable or neither. For example, if the SBU's served market is expected to grow vigorously, this is probably a favorable trend. If market decline is forecast, the trend is probably unfavorable. A level market is usually neither favorable nor unfavorable.

Note that all of the foregoing observations are qualified, because a trend must be viewed in the context of the prior history of the market and the SBU's situation. It is true, for instance, that a flat market is usually viewed as neutral. On the other hand, if the market has been growing prior to the period of the plan and is forecast to flatten out during the planning period, this is clearly unfavorable.

A growing market may also be unfavorable when viewed vis-à-vis the SBU's situation. Consider an SBU that is very strongly positioned in the current generation of a technology but is comparatively weak in the next generation. Regardless of the rate of growth of the market, if the SBU's served market is transitioning to next-generation technology, the SBU is in deep trouble.

With regard to competitors' strategies, at one extreme are those strategies which attack or threaten the SBU; these may be referred to as *offensive* strategies. A competitor's introduction of a product that threatens to eat into the SBU's market share is patently an offensive strategy. At the other extreme are *vulnerable* strategies, which usually result from competitors' neglect of certain segments of the SBU's served market. In between these two extremes are strategies which fall into neither category.

These extremes of market trends and competitors' strategies spawn opportunities or threats for the SBU. The four most dramatic interactions are displayed in Figure 5-2. Opportunities result most frequently from SBU strengths in combination with either a favorable market trend or a vulnerable competitive strategy. Threats arise when the SBU is weak and there is either an unfavorable market trend or an offensive competitive strategy.

Plan For Profitability!

Figure 5-2
Opportunities and Threats

SBU Situation	Market Trend	Competitors' Strategies	?
Strength	Favorable		Opportunity
Strength		Vulnerable	Opportunity
Weakness	Unfavorable		Threat
Weakness		Offensive	Threat

LISTING OPPORTUNITIES AND THREATS

As a first illustration of the concept of Figure 5-2, consider our old friend, the Head Ski Company. This is an example of a company's weakness combining with an unfavorable market trend to pose a threat:

- Company weakness: Insufficient research and development in fiberglass skis

- Unfavorable market trend: Gradual market shift from metal to fiberglass skis

- Threat: Decrease in the demand for metal skis, with potential loss in market share

Here is a more involved example. In the early 1970's, the United States automobile market presented an especially attractive target for foreign automakers, notably the Japanese.

In this situation, there was the double-whammy of a favorable (for the Japanese) market trend and vulnerable (domestic) competitors' strategies. In our frame of reference, the situation may be described as follows:

- Japanese companies' strength: Specialization in small fuel-efficient autos

- Favorable market trend: Increase in the demand for fuel-efficient autos, driven by sharp increases in gasoline prices

- Domestic competitors' vulnerability: Continued emphasis on large autos and lack of emphasis on fuel economy

- Opportunity: Increase in the Japanese companies' share of the United States automobile market

THE LEARNING CURVE

The consolidation of the SBU's opportunities and threats marks that point in the planning process where our focus on the environment transitions from a floodlamp on the market and the competition to a pencil beam on the SBU itself. The remaining steps in the strategic planning process (objectives, strategies, programs, goals, resources and financials) all involve a high degree of introspective activity within the SBU.

Before proceeding to those steps, it is instructive to consider what additional insight may be obtained from the environmental information that we have obtained. Much

116

of this additional perspective is based on the concept of the *learning curve*, which was refined in the 1960's by the Boston Consulting Group[2].

The learning curve is based on a proposition so simplistic that it would seem to be axiomatic. The proposition is that the more units of a product that a manufacturer produces, the cheaper the per-unit cost of manufacture. Thus, the second unit should cost less than the first, the fourth less than the second, the eighth less than the fourth, and so on.

The Boston Consulting Group observed that there was a mathematical correlation between the cumulative volume of units produced and the cost per unit: viz., that every time the cumulative volume of units produced doubles, the manufacturing cost per unit decreases by a fixed percentage for that product. If, for example, the cost per unit declines by 15% each time the cumulative volume of production is doubled, then the product cost is said to exhibit an 85% learning curve.

Three representative learning curves are displayed in Figure 5-3. The steeper the slope of the learning curve, the higher the percentage cost reduction with each doubling in cumulative volume.

The theory of the learning curve does not take into account the effect of inflation. The principle speaks to costs in constant dollar terms, not current dollars. For instance, suppose a product exhibits a 95% learning curve and the cumulative production is doubled over the course of a year. In terms of constant dollars, the cost per unit would be 5% less at the end of the year than at the beginning. How-

---

[2] The Boston Consulting Group, One Boston Place, Boston, Massachusetts

ever, if inflation is running at 7% per year over the same time span, then the cost per unit in current dollars would be 2% higher at year-end than at the beginning of the year.

Figure 5-3
The Learning Curve

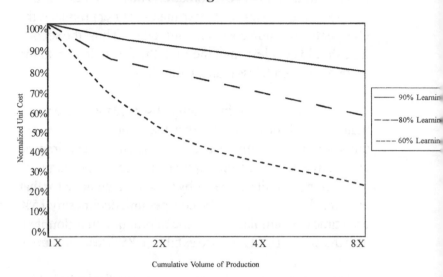

Cumulative Volume of Production

An interesting and somewhat provocative corollary follows from the principle of the learning curve. If several competitors are producing the same product in the same manner, then that competitor with the highest cumulative production volume will have the lowest unit cost of production. As the competitor with the highest cumulative volume, it is also the market share leader. Thus, that competitor with the leading market share has the lowest unit manufacturing cost and is best positioned to increase its market share, to be the most profitable competitor in the market, or both.

As the Boston Consulting Group put it:

Plan For Profitability!

"If experience improves performance, it should follow that the company that has produced the most widgets will be the most efficient widget producer. This implies that market share is vital in determining potential profitability and that new products, whether developed internally or acquired outside, are doomed to lackluster financial performance unless they capture a dominant market position."[3]

Of course, it is absurd to extrapolate the foregoing observation to the conclusion that the company that jumps into the share lead at the genesis of a market will always maintain its lead and have the highest profitability in the market. Nor should you take it on face value that other competitors are permanently "doomed to lackluster financial performance." Most markets are inherently too dynamic to perpetuate such a status quo. Among the fallacies in accepting the proposition that market share is the ultimate deity are the following:

- It does not necessarily follow that the lowest-cost producer offers the lowest price or has the highest profit margins. The lowest-cost producer may be less efficient than its rivals in marketing or management, thus offsetting its inherent cost advantages.

- Except for commodity-like markets, manufacturers seldom produce exactly the same product. Rather, they seek to differentiate their products by special features so that purchasers base their buying decisions on considerations in addition to price.

---

[3] The Boston Consulting Group, Experience Curves as a Planning Tool, 1973

- Ultimately, markets change in character, both in the nature of the products that are available and in the composition of the demand for the products. For example, the lowest-cost producer of mechanical watches was in anything but an enviable position when the watch market began its transition to electronics in the 1970's.

For the above reasons, I do not subscribe to the view that market share is the *only* determinant of success for an SBU. Nonetheless, market share is the most important measure of the SBU's position vis-à-vis its competition.

THE ORIGINAL PORTFOLIO MATRIX

Proceeding from the premise that market share is the most important measure of competitive position, the Boston Consulting Group then addressed the most important measure of market attractiveness, which we concluded in Chapter III was market growth. Again, as with many advances in academic thought, the proposition in retrospect is deceptively simple.

The Boston Consulting Group reasoned that, if market growth and market share are the most important measures of a company's market and position therein, then the best of all worlds is to have a high share of a high-growth market, while the worst situation is to have a small share of a low-growth (or, worse yet, declining) market. This concept eventually evolved into the famous four-block matrix of stars, cash cows, dogs and question marks displayed as Figure 5-4.

Figure 5-4
The Original Portfolio Matrix

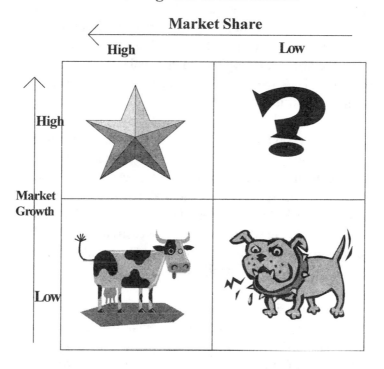

The matrix of Figure 5-4 provides a pictorial means of comparing the positioning of various SBU's within a company (regardless of their diversities of mission and size) according to the key strategic determinants of market share and market growth. In effect, the portfolio matrix provides a snapshot of the relative strategic positioning of the company's portfolio of businesses; hence its name.

The *stars* of the company are in the upper left-hand quadrant (high shares of high-growth markets) and the company's strategy for these businesses should be tailored to keep them so positioned as long as possible. The rub with the stars is that businesses in rapidly expanding markets are notorious devourers of capital, both working and investment. In theory, much of the stars' capital needs should be provided by the *cash cows* in the lower left-hand quadrant. With substantial market shares in low-growth markets, the cash cows have above average profit margins and minimal internal demands for capital. Thus, they should be net generators of cash, most of which is consumed by the stars.

Upon reflection, you may realize that cash cows are nothing more than stars in the twilight of their existence. With reference to the product maturity curve discussed in Chapter III, high-growth markets must inevitably mature, and as the rate of growth declines, the stars slip from the upper left-hand square to the lower where they become cash cows. As such, they begin to return the cash that was plowed into them as stars, hopefully with substantial accrued interest.

In the lower right-hand corner are the *dogs*. Since these businesses are not worthy of investment dollars, most companies harvest them for what meager profits they can generate toward the ultimate end of winding down operations and ultimately closing them down.

The *question marks* in the upper right-hand quadrant are aptly named. In the absence of decisive strategies for these businesses, they will gradually decline into the lower right-hand square, suggesting that inaction breeds dogs. For each question-mark business, the company must decide either to pump investment into the business with the goal of increasing market share and pushing the business to the left toward the star category, or to divest the business and deploy the capital generated by the divestiture among the other businesses in the portfolio.

Plan For Profitability!

Figure 5-5 depicts a typical company's portfolio of five businesses, where the size of each SBU (usually measured in terms of revenues) is indicated by the size of the circle. Although the Boston Consulting Group originally presented rigorous (and complicated) scaling criteria for the x- and y-axes, my preference is to adjust the scalings to fit the variations in market share and growth among the SBU's; such an adaptive scaling is shown in the example.

SBU A is clearly the cash cow of the portfolio of Figure 5-5 and should be providing cash for SBU B (a star) and probably SBU C, which would appear from the display to have the potential to be nudged into the star category. SBU D is a question mark and could be a candidate for divestiture, but such a conclusion requires substantially more insight into the business than that provided by the matrix. Although SBU E is essentially a dog, it still is close enough to the bovine field to suggest that a harvesting strategy is appropriate.

THE NINE-BLOCK MATRIX

General Electric expanded upon the portfolio matrix concept and developed a more comprehensive nine-block matrix to convey comparisons among GE's many SBU's. At first glance, the GE nine-block matrix of Figure 5-6 would appear to be little more than an expansion of the Boston Consulting Group's portfolio matrix from four to nine blocks. Fortunately, for those of us who make a living trying to understand the differences among businesses (with the aim of taking appropriate actions) there is a substantive rationale behind the nine-block matrix.

Figure 5-5
Portfolio Matrix with Quantification of the Axes

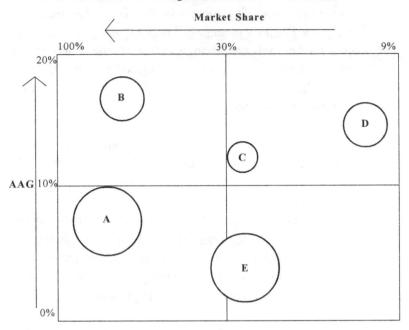

General Electric reasoned that, notwithstanding the importance of market share and market growth, there are many
other factors that must be taken into consideration when trying to compare whether one business is more or less desirable than another. Consequently, GE elevated the matrix dimensions from the single parameters of share and growth to
the multivariate concepts of:

- The *attractiveness* of the industry in which the
  SBU is engaged, and

- The *business strengths* that the SBU has in the
  industry.

Figure 5-6
The Nine-Block Matrix

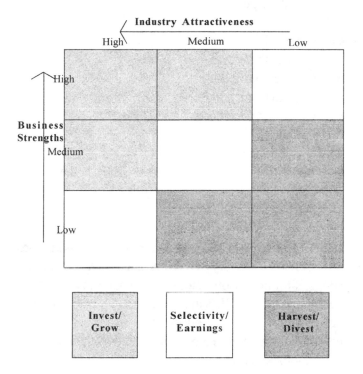

Some of the considerations that enter into the determination of industry attractiveness and SBU business strengths are the following:

Industry Attractiveness
- Market growth
- Market size
- Industry profitability
- Pricing characteristics
- Pricing trends
- Characteristics of the competition
- Vulnerability to inflation

- Cyclicality
- Degree of regulation
- Social image

Business Strengths
- Market share
- Competitive ranking
- Growth history
- Growth expectations
- Profitability
- Brand image
- Beneficial couplings with other SBU's in the company

Moreover, General Electric suggested that it was inappropriate to classify its sundry SBU's into such categories as stars and dogs, if for no reason other than the pejorative connotation associated with SBU's in the latter category. Preferable, in the eyes of GE, was to categorize the businesses according to the generic strategies that were indicated by their locations in the nine-block matrix.

Thus, those SBU's positioned in the three upper left-hand blocks of Figure 5-6 are referred to as *invest/grow* businesses. Those at the other extreme are classified as *harvest/divest* businesses, which is certainly kinder than calling them dogs. Those in the three-block diagonal between the extreme corners are placed in the category of *selectivity/earnings*. These generic classifications determined the tenor of GE's strategic approach to each SBU.

THE ENVIRONMENT OF INTERNATIONAL MICROWIDGETS

One of the techniques that Bill Portes employs in his quest for objectivity in assessing his company's strengths and weaknesses is to ask the opinions of others that know the company well. In this category are not only insiders such as executives and members of the Board of Directors, but also informed outsiders, especially securities analysts, trade association representatives and market researchers that follow the company and its competitors. He then factors these opinions into his own personal assessment. The following is the current assessment of the strengths and weaknesses of International Microwidgets:

Strengths

- Recognized as the pioneer of the modern microwidget

- Leading share of the worldwide market (40%)

- Lowest-cost manufacturer in the market

- Strong financial position

Admittedly, we have not yet discussed the company's financial statements, so you must take the last of the foregoing strengths for the time being on faith. We will discuss the financial statements later in Chapter VIII of this book.

Three areas of weakness are troubling to Portes. These concerns have also been reinforced by external opinions:

1) Although International Microwidgets is the lowest-cost manufacturer, its product margins have been declining. Concurrently, the company's leading competitor, Microwidgets Ichiban, has steadily been improving its margins, aided by its own captive source of microchips. International Microwidgets has traditionally purchased its microchips from external sources at favorable prices because of the volume of its purchases.

2) The regional market with the greatest projected growth over the planning horizon is Asia/Pacific, with an AAG of 20%. Although the company's share of 23% in this region is significant, much of that volume is derived from Japan and Australia and not from the countries in which this dynamic growth is expected to take place. With 55% of the market in this region, Ichiban is far better positioned to reap this new business than is International Microwidgets.

3) Although significantly smaller than the Asia/Pacific market, the market in Eastern Europe is also forecast to grow at 20% per year. Again, International Microwidgets has a respectable share of the market (29%), but Deutsche Microwidgets has twice the presence and an advantageous position foothold in the region because of its proximity and economic ties.

With the foregoing background, you may better appreciate why Portes lists the following three factors as the

Plan For Profitability!

principal weaknesses of his company:

<u>Weaknesses</u>

- Declining improvement in product margins

- Distant second-place share in the Asia/Pacific region (20%)

- Distant second-place share in the Eastern Europe region (29%)

At this point, you may wish to refer back to Figure 5-2 and refresh your memory on how opportunities and threats are produced by the interaction between the controllable environment (a company's own strengths and weaknesses) and the uncontrollable environment (market trends and competitors' strategies). The process is to compare the strengths and weaknesses of International Microwidgets (just discussed) with market trends (discussed in Chapter III) and competitors' strategies (discussed in Chapter IV). One opportunity and four threats practically shout to be articulated as a result of this comparison:

<u>Strength</u>   +   <u>General Widgets Strategy</u>   ⇒   <u>Opportunity</u>
Financial position   Look for a rescuer   Acquire General Widgets

<u>Weakness</u>   +   <u>Ichiban Strategy</u>   ⇒   <u>Threat</u>
Declining margins   Drive down costs   Loss of low-cost leadership

<u>Weakness</u>   +   <u>Ichiban Strategy</u>   ⇒   <u>Threat</u>
Declining margins   Compete by reducing margins Loss of U.S./Canada market share

<u>Weakness</u>   +   Market Trend+<u>Ichiban Strategy</u> ⇒ <u>Threat</u>
Low Asia/Pacific share Rapid growth Dominate the region

<u>Weakness</u>   +   Market Trend+<u>Deutsche Strategy</u> ⇒ <u>Threat</u>
Low E. Europe share Rapid growth   Concentrate on region

In summary, Bill Portes lists the following one opportunity and four threats as paramount in this year's strategic plan:

Opportunity

- Acquisition of General Microwidgets

Threats

- Loss of position as the lowest cost producer to Microwidgets Ichiban

- Loss of market share in the U.S./Canada region to Microwidgets Ichiban

- Loss of market share in the Asia/Pacific region to Microwidgets Ichiban

- Loss of market share in the Eastern Europe region to Deutsche Microwidgets

In the chapters ahead, we shall use the foregoing opportunity and threats as keystones in our development of the strategic plan for International Microwidgets.

SUMMARY

In this chapter, we have discussed the process of distilling our environmental information so that it forms the basis for focusing on the SBU. Some important points to retain about the process of environmental consolidation are:

Plan For Profitability!

- The uncontrollable portion of the environment consists of the market and the competition. The SBU itself is characterized as the controllable element of the environment.

- The SBU should attempt to assess its own strengths and weaknesses in the same manner as it assesses those of its competitors. The challenge is to be objective and to avoid self-delusion.

- The evaluation of the environment (the market, competition and the SBU itself) results in a set of opportunities and threats that confront the SBU. Opportunities and threats arise from interactions between the controllable and the uncontrollable environment.

- Opportunities are spawned when the SBU's strengths coincide with favorable market trends or vulnerable strategies of competitors. Threats arise when SBU weaknesses are juxtaposed with unfavorable market trends or offensive strategies of competitors.

- The learning curve postulates that the unit cost of production decreases with accumulated production volume. It follows from the learning curve that the producer with the leading share of the market is likely to be the lowest-cost producer and therefore the most profitable.

- The Boston Consulting Group's portfolio matrix is a medium by which the various SBU's that comprise a company are positioned according to their relative market shares and market growths to arrive at macro strategic implications. General Electric subsequently refined the concept with its own nine-block matrix that displays industry attractiveness versus business strengths.

If you are developing a strategic plan for your company as you read this material, your challenge now is to articulate your company's strengths and weaknesses as objectively as you can. After that, you are positioned to consolidate the work that you have produced to this point by juxtaposing your description of the uncontrollable environment (the market and the competition) with your assessment of the controllable environment (your company) to arrive at a listing of opportunities and threats that your company faces. Use the techniques that are summarized in Figure 5-2.

If your company has several businesses, at this point you may wish to compare them using one of the matrix concepts of Figures 5-4 through 5-6.

CHAPTER VI

OBJECTIVES, STRATEGIES, PROGRAMS AND GOALS

Football strategy does not originate in a scrimmage.
Walter Lippman, 1914

It is not enough to take steps which may some day lead to a goal; each step must be itself a goal and a step likewise.
Goethe, 1823

The person who makes a success of living is the one who sees his goal steadily and aims for it unswervingly.
Cecil B. de Mille, 1955

As mentioned in the previous chapter, the step of characterizing the environment by developing a concise set of opportunities and threats enables us to narrow our perspective from the global view and concentrate on the SBU itself. We are now able to proceed to the core of the strategic plan, the development of appropriate strategies for the SBU.

This is not an intuitive process; it is an exercise in pure logic. Strategic planning involves assessing the future consequences of current initiatives. Our task is to determine those current actions that will enable the SBU to capitalize on its opportunities and counter its threats.

It is usually enlightening at this point to revisit the mission statement (see Chapter II) and, if necessary, reshape the mission in light of your improved understanding and appreciation of the environment. Recall that the mission statement addresses three questions:

- What are the present characteristics of the business?

- What differentiates the business from its competitors?

- What would we like to see the business become in the future?

As a result of the environmental analysis that you just completed, realistic answers to these questions should be much clearer now than they were at the beginning of the plan. It is particularly revealing to contrast your original perceptions of the business with the environmental realities that have become apparent at this stage in the development of the plan.

In short, changes to the mission statement may be warranted. In keeping with the philosophy that planning is a dynamic and iterative process, these changes should be made.

DEFINITIONS

Moreover, the answer to the third question about the mission can now be expanded into a set of *objectives* for the SBU. Objectives are broad statements of what the SBU intends to accomplish over the planning horizon. Objectives are achieved by *strategies*. Some examples of strategies will be put forth shortly.

Plan For Profitability!

In the context of our approach to planning, strategies are implemented via *programs*. Programs are specific activities that are quantifiable in both cost and duration. Examples of programs include the development of a new product, opening of new sales offices, increasing manufacturing capacity, opening a new product line, discontinuing certain product lines, and so on.

Goals are established to help the SBU measure its progress in the execution of its programs. In contrast to objectives, goals are specific and quantitative. Goals should be expressed in terms of two variables:

- A quantifiable measurement (e.g., dollars, points of market share, achievement of a certain event, and so forth);

- A specific point in time at which the measurement is to be taken.

It should be noted that some practitioners in the field reverse the distinction between objectives and goals. In other words, they define goals as the general statements and objectives as specific. In my view, it makes little difference which convention is used as long as you are consistent throughout the plan and from plan to plan. For our discussion, remember that objectives are the broad aims and goals are the specific. Some examples may serve to clarify the distinction.

The following objective and goal might apply to a start-up business:

- Objective: Become profitable at the earliest possible date.

- Goal: Achieve positive net income, as measured on a quarterly basis, by the seventh quarter after start-up.

Observe that the objective is broad and not very specific. Note also that the goal is derived from the objective and amplifies upon it. In contrast with the objective, the goal is very specific about what has to be accomplished (positive net income) and by when it should be done (seventh quarter after start-up).

Here are an objective and a goal that might pertain to a domestic business with international aspirations:

- Objective: Enter the international market.

- Goal: Establish sales subsidiaries within the next 18 months in, at least, the United Kingdom, Germany, France, Italy, the Benelux and Scandinavia.

Again, note how the objective is deliberately general and lacks any teeth. It would be difficult to measure a CEO's performance against such a nebulous target as "enter the international market." On the other hand, the goal bites down hard on results by quantifying *what* (sales subsidiaries), *where* (the countries cited) and *when* (within 18 months). After 18 months, there would be little room for judgment in appraising the CEO's performance against such concrete measurements.

An objective may propagate more than one goal. Here is an example for a company aiming at leadership in its served market:

- Objective: Achieve the leading share of the served market.

- Goals:
  - ◆ Decrease unit manufacturing cost by 15% from current standards within six months.
  - ◆ Increase the domestic sales force by 50 people by the end of the year.
  - ◆ Increase market share to 40% of total unit shipments within ten quarters.

In this example, an objective gives rise to three goals. In fact, an objective frequently spawns multiple elements of strategy, an element of strategy can result in more than one program, and a program may be measured by several goals. The result is a pyramiding effect, which is covered in more detail in the next section.

Recall that in Chapter II, we discussed the difference between the strategic plan and the operational plan. The point was made there that the strategic plan lays the foundation for the ensuing one-year operational plan. To be more specific, the programs and goals set the stage for this transition from the strategic plan to the operational plan. This point is suggested pictorially by Figure 6-1.

Figure 6-1
Interfaces with the Operational Plan

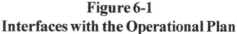
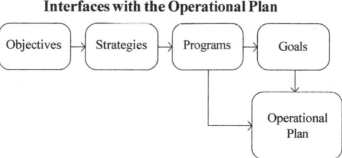

THE PRINCIPLE OF LINKAGES

In my experience, the most productive methodology to derive objectives, strategies, programs and goals is to start by considering each opportunity and threat separately and without regard to other opportunities and threats. My approach is to examine each opportunity or threat in isolation to arrive at one or more objectives that, if accomplished, will capitalize upon the opportunity or counter the threat.

The result is a list of objectives, each of which corresponds to a specific opportunity or threat. At this point, however, the list may contain overlapping or redundant objectives, since each opportunity and threat was considered independently and without regard to its peers. My next step, therefore, is to critique the list of objectives with the aim of eliminating redundancy and overlap and reducing the list to a tight set of objectives for the SBU.

In so doing, it is mandatory that:

● Each opportunity and threat links up with one or more objective;

● Each objective links up with one or more opportunities or threats.

Upon reflection, you will realize the logic behind the foregoing two requirements. If each opportunity and threat is addressed by at least one objective, then there is at least one objective to capitalize on every opportunity and counter every threat. None will have been overlooked. Second, if each objective must be associated with at least one opportunity or threat, then no spurious objectives have crept into the plan. There will be a reason for each objective.

My next step is to follow the same logical process in making the transition from objectives to strategies. In other words, I start by evaluating each objective to the exclusion of the other objectives. The result is a list of strategy alternatives that subsequently needs to be reduced to a concise set of strategies such that:

- Each objective is addressed by at least one element of strategy;

- Each element of strategy supports at least one objective.

The final step is to make the transition from strategies to programs employing the same thought process. Here again we demand that linkages be in place such that:

- Each element of strategy be supported by at least one program;

- Each program relates to at least one element of strategy.

In capsule, this entire process can be distilled into four steps and two rules. The four steps are:

- Opportunities and threats lead to objectives;

- Objectives lead to strategies;

- Strategies lead to goals;

●   Goals lead to programs.

The two rules are:

●   If A leads to B, there must be at least one B for each A;

●   Each B must relate to at least one A.

I refer to this methodology as the *Principle of Linkages*. To illustrate the principle of linkages graphically, refer to the decision tree of Figure 6-2. Assume for the moment that we are analyzing opportunities and threats to derive objectives and that our attention is focused upon Opportunity 3 to the total exclusion of Opportunities 1 and 2 and Threats 1, 2 and 3. There are two Objectives, 1 and 2, that can be postulated as appropriate responses to Opportunity 3. After some consideration, we conclude that Objective 2 is the better of the two and Objective 1 is discarded.

To realize Objective 2, three alternative strategies are proposed and we select Strategies 1 and 3 as the best courses of action. To implement Strategy 1, we adopt Program 1, which will be measured by Goal 2. Programs 3 and 4, which will be measured by Goals 4 and 5, respectively, will implement strategy 3.

The success of this methodology lies on adopting a philosophy that I call *flexible rigor*. (I recognize that this has the hallmarks of an oxymoron, but bear with me for a moment while I explain.) The *rigor* is embodied in the requirement that there be no dead ends to the decision tree of Figure 6-2, i.e., that there be at least one clear path or *linkage* from each opportunity and threat on the left-hand side of the tree to the goals on the right-hand side. This dictates that at least one objective follows from each opportunity or threat, that the objective generates at least one element of strategy, and so on.

Figure 6-2
The Concept of Linkages

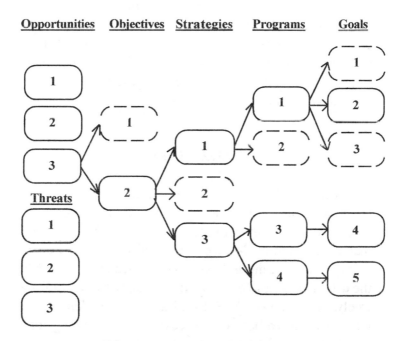

The sole exception to this rule is where the strategy is one of deliberate inaction (i.e., deliberately do nothing). In this case, there is clearly no activity (program) and the decision tree is permitted to truncate without a complete set of linkages through to the goals.

On the other hand, the planner must be *flexible* enough to realize that, since there are usually interrelationships among opportunities and threats, there will probably be couplings among the resulting objectives, strategies, programs and goals. Hence, consideration of each opportunity and threat to the total exclusion of its companions is likely to yield objectives, strategies, programs and goals that overlap, are redundant or even contradict one another.

Obviously then, after decision trees such as that of Figure 6-2 have been developed for each opportunity and threat, they must be combined to eliminate overlapping or redundant elements and to reconcile contradictory conclusions. The result of this reconciliation is an integrated set of objectives, strategies, programs and goals, the linkages among which are evident and explicit. See Figure 6-3.

OBJECTIVES

In the early 1980's, Advanced Pumping Systems, Inc. (APS) was a developmental-stage Colorado-based company that had designed and was attempting to manufacture and market an advanced oil-well pumping unit of universal design. Pumping units are those aboveground structures that provide the driving power to draw oil from wells that do not flow freely. According to APS, by adjusting stroke length and interchanging gearboxes, its three models of pumping units could supersede 39 discrete models of its competitors.

Plan For Profitability!

Figure 6-3
Interrelationships among Linkages

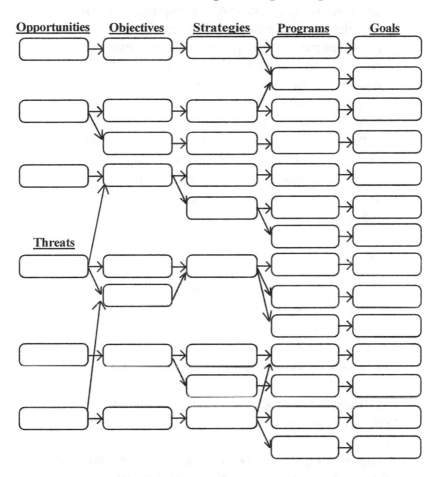

You will recall that we have encountered APS several times so far. The mission of APS, originally presented in Chapter II, was as follows:

Advanced Pumping Systems designs and markets universally adaptable oil pumping units to oil industry customers in the United States. Founded in 1981, APS is an innovator in the design of oil pumping equipment with distinctive operational simplicity, versatility, and cost effectiveness. Three APS pumping units have been designed to handle the full range of gear requirements that previously required ten times as many different-sized conventional units. In addition, APS has designed technically innovative oil well simulation and analysis equipment that can provide accurate performance data on its competitors' units as well as its own. APS plans to stay at the leading edge of pumping unit design by implementing remote monitoring capabilities to existing units and by designing a highly advanced electronic pumping unit that should revolutionize the industry.

The prices of APS's pumping units varied according to size and capacity, and ranged from $19,000 per unit to $68,000 per unit, with an average price of $48,000 per unit. The served market of APS, displayed in Chapter III (Figure 3-5), was estimated at some 25,000 units per year, which equates to $1.2 billion annually. Demand was projected to be essentially level through the planning horizon.

Although there were several dozen manufacturers of pumping units, four major competitors commanded three-quarters of the served market, which is shown as one of the examples in Chapter IV (Figure 4-5). Dominating the market was Lufkin Industries, with a market share that was twice that of the second leading supplier. At the time of this analysis, APS had not shipped any pumping units to customers.

In early 1983, Advanced Pumping Systems developed its first strategic plan. After some deliberation, the company concluded that the environment that they faced could be distilled into four opportunities and three threats. The four opportunities were:

- *Complacent Competition*: With one exception, the major competitors in the pumping unit market had not changed for decades. Their market shares had not shifted markedly for five years and the designs of their pumping units were old. There was clearly room for APS to capture a share of this market against this complacent set of competitors.

- *Customer Flexibility*: Customers for pumping units customarily preferred not to restrict their purchases to a single manufacturer but to buy from two or more sources. The opportunity existed for APS to become qualified as an alternative source on customers' supplier lists.

- *Demonstrable Economic Savings*: Among the advantages of the APS universal design were the cost savings that could be realized by its users. These savings manifested themselves in two ways:

  - By virtue of its adjustability and the interchangeability of its gear boxes, each APS pumping unit could be optimally tuned to the unique conditions of the well upon which it was operating, thereby requiring some 35% less pumping energy than conventional units.

  - Since three APS models covered the range of applications of 39 competitive units, customers could carry a far smaller inventory of pumping units for their well pumping needs.

- *Geographical Location*: The competitors of APS were located in or in close proximity to the lucrative oil fields of Western Texas. Located in Colorado, APS was close enough to the Texas fields to serve them without major handicap, but also was situated at the heart of the emerging Rocky Mountain oil fields.

The three threats that faced the company were as follows:

- *Insufficient Resources for Growth*: Since its formation in 1981, APS had been operating on a shoe string. Its principal sources of working capital consisted of sporadic contributions of equity capital from local investors, loans from and salary deferrals by employees, proceeds from a $900,000 limited research and development partnership, and a generous (and exhausted) line of credit from a local bank. Without a substantial infusion of capital (estimated at $3.5 million), APS could not proceed from development to marketing and manufacturing.

- *Oppressive Debt*: In addition to the lack of growth capital, in two years of operation, APS had burdened itself with about $1 million in debt, chiefly trade payables. Accounts payable were up to nine months overdue and creditors were becoming increasingly vociferous in their demands for payment. The specter of having to close the doors was ever present.

●   *Insufficient Management Talent*: The founders
and driving forces of Advanced Pumping Systems were three individuals with skills in Engineering, Manufacturing and Sales. Totally missing from the management team was expertise in
Marketing, Finance and General Management.
It was unlikely that APS could survive, much less
move forward, without these critical disciplines.

Recall that *objectives* are broad, general statements of
what the company wants to accomplish. After considering
the foregoing four opportunities and three threats, the founders
of Advanced Pumping Systems were able to condense the
company's objectives into five succinct statements, as follows:

●   Conserve capital to the fullest extent possible.

●   Obtain sufficient capital for, first, immediate sur-
vival and, then, long-term growth.

●   Field a first-class management team.

●   Convince potential customers of the advantages
of the APS pumping unit.

●   Confine initial marketing activities to the Western
United States.

Figure 6-4 shows how these five objectives link to their
predecessor opportunities and threats. Note that, in accordance with the Principle of Linkages, each opportunity and
threat leads to at least one objective and each

objective supports at least one opportunity or threat.

STRATEGIES

Strategies are broad statements of how the company intends to pursue its objectives. The articulation of the preceding five clear objectives led APS to the realization that its strategies could be expressed in terms of seven elements:

- Subcontract all manufacturing and assembly operations at the outset to minimize initial requirements for capital.

- Explore venture capital sources for immediate financing, with emphasis on local sources with expertise in the oil industry.

- Cultivate local brokerage houses to prepare for second-round financing via a public offering of shares.

- Identify the top management team and be prepared to bring them aboard when venture capital funding is committed.

- Focus on those potential customers with the highest probability of payoff (the major oil companies).

- Test the APS pumping unit on production oil wells in head-to-head comparisons with competitive units.

- Concentrate marketing activities in the swath of oil fields from Wyoming to Texas.

Figure 6-4
Linkages between Opportunities/Threats and Objectives

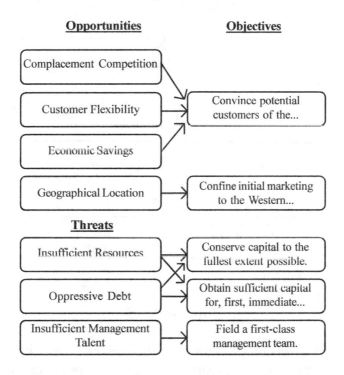

Figure 6-5 depicts the linkages between APS's five objectives and seven elements of strategy. Note again that the two rules governing linkages are followed to the letter. Each objective leads to at least one element of strategy and each element of strategy supports at least one objective.

Figure 6-5
Linkages between Objectives and Strategies

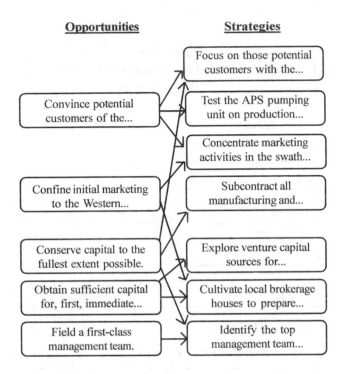

PROGRAMS

Programs are specific activities that are organized to implement the various elements of strategy. Advanced Pumping Systems instituted seven major programs:

- Customer Visitation: Planned contacts with the decision makers at the major oil companies.

- Product Promotion: Publicity about the APS pumping unit, including product brochures, audio-visual demonstrations, features in trade journals, attendance at trade shows and papers at technical symposia.

- Test Installations: Installation of the APS pumping unit on producing wells of potential customers, monitoring of the production data and comparison of the data with that of competitors' pumping units.

- Subcontract Manufacturing: Negotiation of terms and conditions with subcontractors, preferably in the local area.

- Business Plans: Preparation of a five-year strategic plan and a one-year operational plan for subsequent review with potential venture capital sources and brokers.

- Capital Sourcing: Carefully planned exposure of the APS business case to venture capital sources and public brokerage firms, with subsequent follow-through and closing to obtain the capital.

- Executive Interviews: Interviews of candidates for Chief Executive Officer, Chief Financial Officer and Vice President of Marketing, and selection of the leading candidates.

See Figure 6-6 for the linkages between the APS's strategies and programs.

Figure 6-6
Linkages between Strategies and Programs

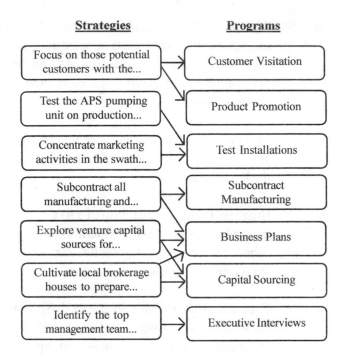

Strategies	Programs
Focus on those potential customers with the...	Customer Visitation
Test the APS pumping unit on production...	Product Promotion
Concentrate marketing activities in the swath...	Test Installations
Subcontract all manufacturing and...	Subcontract Manufacturing
Explore venture capital sources for...	Business Plans
Cultivate local brokerage houses to prepare...	Capital Sourcing
Identify the top management team...	Executive Interviews

GOALS

Goals are those measures by which the company intends to monitor its progress in the execution of its programs. APS set nine goals for itself, covering the three-year time span from early 1983 through the end of 1985, as follows:

- Complete the 1983-88 strategic plan and the 1983-84 operational plan in the first quarter of 1983.

- Initiate at least two pumping unit test installations on potential customers' wells by mid-1983.

152

Plan For Profitability!

- Obtain purchase orders and realize initial revenues in 1983.

- Select the CEO, CFO and Marketing executive by the fourth quarter of 1983.

- Obtain at least $2 million in venture capital funding prior to the end of 1983.

- Achieve manufacturing margins of 20% in 1983 and 35% in 1984.

- Realize at least $6 million in revenues in 1984.

- Tender a $6 million public offering at the beginning of 1985.

- Achieve profitability, measured on a quarterly basis, by the fourth quarter of 1985.

See Figure 6-7. Of course, the foregoing objectives, strategies, programs and goals represent the end product of the linkage procedure described earlier in this chapter. I have spared you the exercise (which APS went through) of plowing through the methodology that ultimately yielded the linkage trees shown in Figures 6-4 through 6-7.

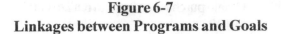

Figure 6-7
Linkages between Programs and Goals

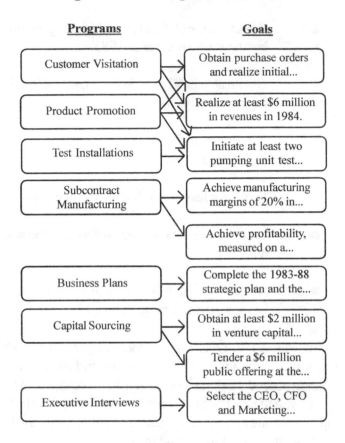

INTERNATIONAL MICROWIDGETS

As we left International Microwidgets in the last chapter, Bill Portes had decided to highlight one opportunity and four threats in this year's strategic plan. They are repeated below:

<u>Opportunity</u>

● Acquisition of General Microwidgets

Plan For Profitability!

<u>Threats</u>

- Loss of position as the lowest cost producer to Microwidgets Ichiban

- Loss of market share in the U.S./Canada region to Microwidgets Ichiban

- Loss of market share in the Asia/Pacific region to Microwidgets Ichiban

- Loss of market share in the Eastern Europe region to Deutsche Microwidgets

Opportunities and threats generate objectives, which, you will recall, are broad statements of what the company intends to accomplish over the horizon of the plan. In the case of International Microwidgets, the objectives are fairly straightforward. There are four of them. Their linkages with the opportunities and threats are shown in Figure 6-8.

- *Acquire General Widgets*: This objective is the obvious result of the opportunity to acquire the company. It also will help the counter the threat of loss of share in the U.S./Canada market since the bulk of General Widgets' revenues derive from its home market.

- *Improve product margins*: This objective will clearly assist in countering all four threats that the company faces.

Figure 6-8
Opportunities/Threats-Objectives Linkages
for International Microwidgets

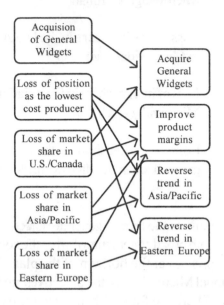

● *Reverse the trend of decreasing market share in the Asia/Pacific region*: This is a forthright counter to the threat of loss of market share in the region. One of the strategies for realizing this objective, as we will see momentarily, is to assemble microwidgets in the region in a country where the cost of assembly is less than in the United States. Not only will the cost of product be reduced, but also the aura of local manufacture should augur well for increased revenues in the region.

● *Reverse the trend of decreasing market share in the Eastern Europe region*: The same comments apply here as for the Asia/Pacific region.

Plan For Profitability!

Every year when Bill Portes revisits his strategic business plan, he prods himself to avoid doing "business as usual." You are certainly familiar with the saying, "If it ain't broke, don't fix it." In technology businesses, nothing could be farther from the truth. With the pace of technological change, by the time it is broke, it may be too late to fix it.

My experience is that an unfavorable trend will continue unabated unless action is taken to correct it. This year, two interrelated unfavorable trends disturb Portes: (1) the loss of market share in three geographical regions and (2) the steady improvement in Ichiban's margins coupled with declining improvements in his own company's margins. Clearly, decisive steps need to be taken to improve manufacturing costs.

One of the factors underlying the declining costs of Microwidgets Ichiban is that the Japanese company belongs to a consortium (or *zaibatsu* in Japanese) that also includes a major semiconductor company. In effect, Ichiban has its own captive source of microchips, with very favorable pricing. In contrast, International Microwidgets has always purchased its microchips from external sources, relying on competitive bidding and the volume of its purchases to keep its costs low. This year, Portes has made a major decision: to manufacture microchips rather than buy them. This entails a significant capital investment in a semiconductor manufacturing facility.

Heretofore, International Microwidgets has assembled all of its microwidgets in the United States. In another dramatic move, Bill Portes decides to establish two new assembly plants, one in China to serve the Asia/Pacific region and another in Eastern Europe to serve both Eastern and Western Europe. Not only will lower labor costs in these regions reduce the cost of assembly, but the perception of local manufacture may also have a favorable influence on market share

157

in the regions.

In summary, Portes decides on four principal elements of strategy for this year's strategic plan. Their linkages with objectives are shown in Figure 6-9:

● Acquire General Widgets.

● Manufacture microchips internally.

● Assemble in the Asia/Pacific region.

● Assemble in Eastern Europe.

Figure 6-9
Objectives-Strategies Linkages
for International Microwidgets

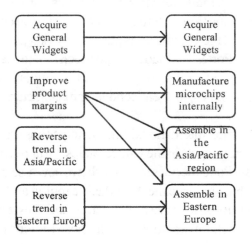

Plan For Profitability!

Portes estimates that, if a deal can be cut to acquire General Widgets, it should be complete by the middle of the next year (Year 1). He also targets to bring the new semiconductor plant and both assembly plants on line by the end of the year. For International Microwidgets, the linkages from strategies to programs and from programs to goals are all one-to-one linkages. The programs and goals are summarized in Figure 6-10.

Figure 6-10
Programs and Goals for International Microwidgets

Program	Goal
Acquisition of General Widgets Year 1: mid-year	
Semiconductor Manufacturing Plant	Year 1: year-end
Asia/Pacific Assembly Plant	Year 1: year-end
Eastern Europe Assembly Plant Year 1: year-end	

SUMMARY

Here are the highlights of Chapter VI:

- Before proceeding to objectives, strategies, programs and goals, it is helpful to review the mission statement against the background of your improved understanding of the environment.

- Objectives are broad statements of what the SBU intends to accomplish over the planning horizon. Strategies are broad descriptions of how the SBU plans to achieve its objectives.

- Programs are specific activities to execute strategies. Goals are quantifiable measurements of the progress of programs. Programs and goals constitute the interface between the strategic plan and the operational plan.

- There should be a logical flow or linkage from the opportunities and threats through to the goals of the strategic plan. Specifically, objectives should flow from opportunities and threats, strategies should flow from objectives, programs from strategies, and goals from programs.

Now is the time for you to methodically step through the process of developing objectives, strategies, programs and goals for your company. Starting with the opportunities and threats that you identified at the end of the last chapter, consider each one in isolation of the others and propose one or more objectives to capitalize on the opportunity or counter the threat. Then, refine the objectives to eliminate redundancies and overlaps until you can draw a linkage tree from the opportunities and threats to the objectives in the same manner as shown in Figure 6-4.

Continue the process from objectives to strategies, from strategies to programs and from programs to goals with the aim of producing concise linkage trees like those in Figures 6-5 through 6-7. These four elements, objectives, strategies, programs and goals, form the basis for the detailed resources and financial projections that follow, and the latter two, programs and goals, are the initial foundation for the annual operating plan.

CHAPTER VII

RESOURCES

Much of our American progress has been the product of the individual who had an idea; pursued it; fashioned it; tenaciously clung to it against all odds; and then produced it, sold it, and profited from it.

Hubert H. Humphrey, 1966

Understanding . . . needs is half the job of meeting them.

Adlai Stevenson, 1952

In this chapter, we will discuss the penultimate element of the strategic plan, the *resources* required to execute the activities of the plan. These resources may be segregated into two categories:

- Those resources that are required to sustain the operation of the SBU. These may be viewed as a core set of resources that would be required to run the company even if the strategy were to maintain the status quo.

- An incremental set of resources that are required to implement the SBU's strategy. These resources flow from the programs identified in the last chapter.

Resources consist of:

- Personnel

- Facilities (property and plant)

- Equipment.

Resources must, of course, be paid for, which means that personnel, facilities and equipment must ultimately be translated into dollars. We will consider these translations later in this chapter. For the moment, suffice it to say that the cost of people flows directly to the operating statement in the form of expenses for salaries, wages and benefits, while facilities and equipment costs flow both to the operating statement and the balance sheet (for leased and capitalized items). This should become clearer as we proceed.

PEOPLE

The most important resource in the strategic plan is usually *people*. The cost of people consists of salaries, wages, bonuses, fringe benefits and related items. In the companies with which I have been associated over my career, people costs have typically comprised as much as one-third of total revenues. Although this figure varies from industry to industry and even among companies in the same industry, it underscores the importance of accurately projecting people requirements and their associated costs.

The basic unit of people projections is commonly referred to as *headcount*. To arrive at consolidated people costs, the first step is to segment the headcount into skill categories or job classifications. Figures 7-1 and 7-2 depict the headcount projection by job type for a Fortune 500 company.

Figure 7-1
Worldwide Personnel by Job Type

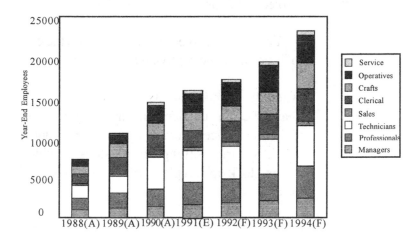

Figure 7-2
Worldwide Personnel by Job Type
(Year-End Employees)

	1989(A)	1990(A)	1991(A)	1992(E)	1993(F)	1994(F)	1995(F)	AAG
Managers	750	1,186	1,489	1,706	1,796	1,964	2,339	21%
Professionals	1,376	2,160	2,872	3,409	3,615	4,048	4,870	23
Technicians	1,781	2,795	3,951	4,262	4,531	5,011	5,968	22
Sales	162	253	334	375	402	441	525	22
Clerical	1,155	1,808	2,356	2,659	2,800	3,106	3,676	21
Crafts	1,045	1,642	1,626	1,943	2,101	2,305	2,745	17
Operatives	1,023	1,599	2,447	2,577	2,725	3,006	3,557	23
Service	59	92	122	136	144	160	191	22
Total	7,351	11,535	15,197	17,047	18,023	20,041	23,871	22%

To make the conversion from headcount to dollars of personnel expense, it is necessary to consider:

●   The mean salary or wage rate in each category or classification

- Anticipated overtime and shift premiums

- Projected bonuses and commissions

- Anticipated turnover of employees and the cost of hiring new and replacement employees

- The cost of fringe benefits, i.e., vacation pay, sick leave, medical and dental insurance, life and accident insurance, unemployment compensation, social security, savings plans, stock purchase plans, stock option plans, retirement plans and so on.

FACILITIES

The second major category of resources is *facilities*, viz., land and buildings, especially the latter which is referred to as *plant*. The basic measurement of plant is area, which is typically expressed in terms of square feet. Figures 7-3 and 7-4 are projections of worldwide plant space for the same company as that of Figures 7-1 and 7-2.

One of the tests to determine if the plant space projections are reasonable is to calculate the average floor space per employee. For the company described in Figures 7-1 through 7-4, floor space per employee is arrived at simply by dividing total floor space (Figure 7-4) by total employees (Figure 7-2). A rule of thumb for light manufacturing firms is for floor space to average between 200 and 250 square feet per employee. Displayed in Figure 7-5, our typical company varies between 215 and 246 square feet per employee over the planning period.

Plan For Profitability!

Figure 7-3
Worldwide Floor Space

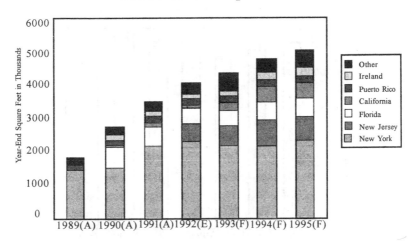

Figure 7-4
Worldwide Floor Space
(Year-End Floor Space in Thousands)

	1989(A)	1990(A)	1991(A)	1992(E)	1993(F)	1994(F)	1995(F)	AAG
New York	1492	1617	2140	2338	2137	2135	2235	7%
New Jersey		10	470	602	902	902		
Florida	435	482	402	402	402	402		
California	68	82	95	263	429	437		
Puerto Rico	86	142	164	164	164	164	164	11
Ireland	146	146	146	146	296	296		
Other	155	255	346	410	500	600	700	29
Total	1733	2633	3370	4025	4214	4928	5136	20%

Figure 7-5
Facility Space per Employee

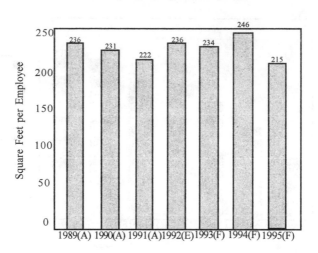

Of course, the validity test of space per employee can be applied below the gross corporate level to any of the company's plant sites. All that is required is a breakdown of employees per location such as that depicted by Figures 7-6 and 7-7. Comparison of the data of these figures with the space per location of Figures 7-3 and 7-4 readily yields the average space per employee at each plant site.

The validity check of floor space per employee provides a coarse indication of how efficiently a company's plant space is being utilized. Of perhaps more importance is the question: how efficiently are the people being utilized? The validity test most frequently employed to answer this question at the macro level is revenues per employee, i.e., revenues divided by the total number of employees. This indicator should generally increase over the planning period because:

166

Plan For Profitability!

- Selling prices will generally increase with time due to the effects of inflation;

- The number of employees required to produce and market a given volume of products should decrease with time in accordance with the learning curve.

Figure 7-6
Worldwide Personnel by Job Site

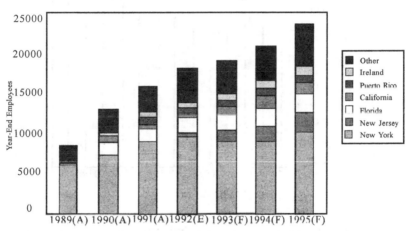

Figure 7-7
Worldwide Personnel by Job Site
(Year-End Employees)

	1989(A)	1990(A)	1991(A)	1992(E)	1993(F)	1994(F)	1995(F)	AAG
New York	5,430	6,486	8,393	9,097	8,705	8,822	10,500	12%
New Jersey				260	1,014	1,306	2,618	
Florida		1,290	1,645	1,621	1,682	1,915	2,030	
California	25	44	223	357	672	896	1,115	88
Puerto Rico	188	627	696	678	705	770	825	28
Ireland		284	435	650	700	850	1,000	
Other	1,708	2,804	3,805	4,384	4,545	5,482	5,783	23
Total	7,351	11,535	15,197	17,047	18,023	20,041	23,871	22%

Figure 7-8 is a representative plot of revenues per employee for the same company depicted in Figures 7-1 through 7-7. Note the generally increasing trend of revenues per employee in this figure.

Figure 7-8
Revenues per Employee

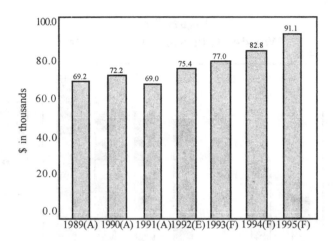

As with headcount, the cost of facilities must be converted into dollars for inclusion in the financial statements. A major consideration in this conversion is whether the facilities are purchased or leased. Purchased facilities (i.e., facilities owned by the company) result in non-cash depreciation charges against the operating statement, whereas leased facilities are reflected in rental payments. In addition to depreciation or lease payments, facilities projections should also include such occupancy-related items as taxes, insurance, utilities, telecommunications, custodial and security services, and related costs.

EQUIPMENT

The third major component of resources is *equipment*, which can range from ordinary items such as office furniture to expensive and sophisticated equipment such as fully automated production lines. Most companies have a dollar threshold below which they expense all purchased equipment. Above the threshold, equipment is referred to as *capital equipment*, which merely refers to the practice of booking the equipment as a capital asset (if purchased) and depreciating it over time in accordance with relevant depreciation schedules. Alternatively, capital equipment may be leased.

TRANSITION TO THE FINANCIAL STATEMENTS

Ultimately, resource projections flow into the financial statements as projected costs of doing business. We will delve into financial statements in the next chapter. Suffice it to say at this point that there are three fundamental financial statements with which we are concerned in strategic planning:

- The *operating statement*, also called the profit-and-loss (P&L) statement, which depicts the company's revenues, expenses and profit for each fiscal year over the period of the strategic plan;

- The *balance sheet*, which is a summary of the company's assets, liabilities and net worth at the end of each year of the plan;

- The statement of *sources and uses of funds*, which summarizes how cash was generated and how it was spent in each year of the plan.

Figure 7-9 illustrates the significant interactions between the resource projections and the financial statements.

Figure 7-9
The Resources-Financials Interrelationship

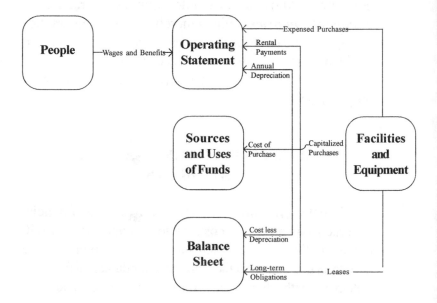

As shown in Figure 7-9, personnel projections flow directly to the operating statement as the cost of salaries, wages and benefits. The flow of facilities and equipment, however, depends on whether they are purchased or leased.

When facilities and equipment are purchased, the major impacts are on the funds flow statement, where capital purchases are reflected as uses of funds, and on the balance sheet, where the purchases appear as capital assets. Consequently, depreciation charges appear on the operating statement and are accrued on the balance sheet.

Plan For Profitability!

In the case of leased facilities and equipment, the major interface is with the operating statement. In some cases, long-term facility lease obligations must also be reflected as liabilities on the balance sheet.

RESOURCE PROJECTIONS

In 1985, Industrial Terminal Systems Corporation (ITS) was a struggling start-up manufacturer of computer terminals for harsh factory environments. The company was attempting to obtain $2 million in equity capital from the venture capital community. How that precise figure was derived will be explained in the next chapter.

As a precursor to contacting venture capitalists, ITS prepared a five-year strategic plan for potential investors. I have chosen to use this small company as an example because its resource projections are relatively simple yet illustrate all of the fundamentals of the build-up of resource projections and their subsequent translation into financial statements.

To further simplify the example and avoid the clutter of nine years of financial history and projections, we shall focus on only three years: the year in which the plan was prepared (1985) and the first two years of projections (1986-87). It was in this time frame, incidentally, that the company predicted that it would consume the equity capital, turn profitable and achieve positive cash flow.

The company's first step was to forecast its headcount needs. This tabulation is shown in Figure 7-10. It is important to realize that this spreadsheet was iterated several times during the planning exercise, but it was the starting point.

171

Note that the headcount forecast is divided into three categories: General and Administrative (G&A), Marketing and Sales, and Operations (Engineering and Manufacturing). ITS projected that its headcount would increase from its then-current level of three employees at the end of 1985 to 20 at year-end 1986 and 37 at year-end 1987.

Figure 7-10 is a tabulation of the average headcount in each year, not the year-end figure. ITS's planned ramp-up in headcount resulted in projected average annual headcount of 12.0 and 30.5 in 1986 and 1987, respectively. Most of the employees were to be housed at the company's headquarters, with a few field sales personnel stationed elsewhere in the United States.

As shown in Figure 7-10, the company used its headcount forecast to size its needs for its headquarters facility. Assuming 250 square feet per employee and allowing some margin for error, the company forecast that it could start with a modest headquarters facility of 2500 square feet, but would need to expand to 5000 square feet by mid-1986 and to 10,000 square feet in mid-1987.

We have yet to introduce the derivation of the company's revenue projections. That will be done in the next chapter, but the resulting ITS revenue projections are displayed as a memo item on the next-to-last line of Figure 7-10. Note that revenues were projected to increase from a nominal amount in 1985 to $1.81 million in 1986 and $10.67 million in 1987. This memo line permits us to calculate the validity check on employee utilization, revenues per employee. Observe that revenues increase from zero to $151,000 per employee in 1986 and to $350,000 per employee in 1987.

172

Figure 7-10
People and Facilities Projections

Headcount (Yearly Average)	1985(E)	1986(F)	1987(F)
General and Administrative			
President/General Manager	1.00	1.00	1.00
Controller	0.00	0.50	1.00
MIS Manager	0.00	0.00	0.50
Receivables Manager	0.00	0.00	0.25
Administration	1.00	1.25	3.25
	2.00	2.75	6.00
Marketing and Sales			
Marketing Manager	0.00	1.00	1.00
Product Marketing	0.00	0.75	1.75
Customer Service	0.00	0.75	2.25
Field Sales	0.00	1.00	3.25
Administration	0.00	0.50	1.00
	0.00	4.00	9.25
Operations			
Operations Manager	1.00	1.00	1.00
Engineers	0.00	2.00	7.25
Production	0.00	1.75	6.00
Administration	0.00	0.50	1.00
	1.00	5.25	15.25
Total Employees	3.00	12.00	30.50
Less Field Employees	0.00	1.00	3.25
Total Headquarter Employees	3.00	11.00	27.25
Headquarters Floor Space (square feet at year-end)	1,000	5,000	10,000
Floor Space per Employee	333	455	367
Revenues ($ in thousands)	-	1,808	10,665
Revenues per Employee ($ in thousands)	0	151	350

173

Hence, revenues per employee were projected to increase, a favorable sign. However, revenues of $350,000 per employee were, in 1987, an extremely high figure for a company like ITS. The company explained this by calling attention to its strategy of subcontracting the entire manufacturing of its products to outside vendors, thereby obviating the need for a large manufacturing organization. Nevertheless, in my opinion, it was questionable whether any company could, at that time, sustain almost $11 million of revenues with only 31 average annual employees (37 at year-end). This concern, incidentally, was also shared by prospective investors.

The next step is to translate the headcount projections of Figure 7-10 into dollars. Figure 7-11 represents the conversion of the G&A headcount forecast into monetary terms.

There are, of course, spreadsheets comparable to that of Figure 7-11 for Marketing and Sales and for Operations, but I have excluded them in the interest of brevity. A few aspects of these calculations are worthy of note:

- The salary projections allowed for merit or cost-of- living increases at periodic intervals.

- Fringe benefits were calculated at 25% of salaries and wages. This was representative of the cost of these benefits at the time that these projections were developed.

- Travel expenses were also estimated at a fixed percentage of salaries and wages. The percentage, however, was dependent upon how much business travel was associated with the functional category. At one extreme, Marketing and Sales was allocated 20% of salaries and wages to travel,

while at the other, Operations was budgeted a
mere 2%.

Figure 7-11
G&A Expense
($ except as noted)

	1985(E)	1986(F)	1987(F)
Salaries and Wages			
President/General Manager	80,000	120,000	120,000
Controller	-	24,000	50,400
MIS Manager	-	-	20,000
Receivables Manager	-	-	7,500
Administration	15,000	22,500	26,900
	95,000	166,500	260,900
Other Expenses			
Benefits (1)	23,750	41,625	65,225
Travel and Living (2)	7,600	13,320	20,872
Telephone (3)	2,850	4,995	7,827
Office Supplies	1,000	1,665	2,565
Insurance	3,000	4,500	9,000
Professional Services	9,500	16,500	27,000
Ad Valorem Taxes (4)	-	3,616	21,330
	47,700	86,221	153,819
Total G&A Expenses	142,700	252,721	414,719

Notes: (1) 25% of Salaries and Wages
(2) 8% of Salaries and Wages
(3) 3% of Salaries and Wages
(4) 0.2% of Revenues

Figure 7-12 summarizes the bottom line expenses for
G&A, Marketing and Sales, and Operations. Validity tests
can also be applied to each of these categories of expense, as
illustrated by the calculations at the bottom of the figure. G&A
expenses, for example, level off at 4% of revenues in 1987,
which is indicative of an extremely lean G&A structure. Operations expenses constitute only 9% of revenues in 1987,

which is also meager and suggests that ITS may have under-stated its projected Engineering needs. The Marketing and Sales forecast of 16% of revenues in 1987 is likewise austere for this type of market. All of these observations support the previous observation that the company's headcount projec-tions may have been understated.

Figure 7-12
Summary of People Expense
($ except as noted)

	1985(E)	1986(F)	1987(F)
Expenses			
Marketing and Sales	39,500	542,634	1,687,934
Operations	202,400	321,410	932,660
G&A	142,700	252,721	414,719
Revenues ($ in thousands)	-	1,808	10,665
Expenses/Revenues			
Marketing and Sales		30%	16%
Operations		18%	9%
G&A		14%	4%

The projected expense for facilities flows directly from the facilities projections of Figure 7-10. Most start-up compa-nies lease their facilities at the outset, as was the case with ITS. The company estimated that it could obtain adequate space for an all-inclusive amount of $12 per square foot. You will recall that the company planned to start with 2500 square feet (the space that it was occupying at the time), expand to 5000 square feet in mid-1986, and expand again to 10,000 square feet in mid-1987. Figure 7-13 contains a tabulation of the resulting projections for facilities expense.

Figure 7-13
Summary of Facilities Expense
($ except as noted)

	1985(E)	1986(F)	1987(F)
Floor Space (Yearly average square feet)	1,000	3,750	7,500
Facilities Expense (at $12 per square foot)	12,000	45,000	90,000

Completing the trio of people, plant and equipment resources, ITS made a detailed projection its equipment needs over the planning horizon. The company planned to buy all of its planned equipment. Contained in Figure 7-14 is a summary of the equipment projections. They are modest, but this is not surprising since the company, as mentioned earlier, planned to subcontract its manufacturing and thus avoid the need for a substantial investment in production equipment. Depreciation is also shown as a memo to the capital equipment listing; the company assumed straight-line depreciation over a period of five years.

Figure 7-14
Summary of Equipment Expense
($ except as noted)

	1985(E)	1986(F)	1987(F)
Office Equipment and Furnishings	-	59,000	53,000
Laboratory Equipment	10,000	26,000	26,000
Production Equipment	10,000	57,000	68,000
Leasehold Improvements	-	10,000	10,000
Total	20,000	152,000	157,000
Depreciation	4,000	34,400	65,800

INTERNATIONAL MICROWIDGETS

When we left International Microwidgets in the last chapter, Bill Portes had decided to embark upon an ambitious plant expansion program with the goal of having two new assembly plants, one in Eastern Europe and the other in China, and a new semiconductor plant in the United States operational by the end of next year (Year 1). He estimates that the cost of bringing all three plants on line will be slightly more than $200 million. Figure 7-15 shows the history and his forecast of expenditures for property, plant and equipment.

Figure 7-15
International Microwidgets
Property, Plant and Equipment
($ in millions)

Year	-2(A)	-1(A)	0(E)	1(F)	2(F)	3(F)
Property	0	0	0	10	0	0
Plant	0	0	0	100	0	0
Equipment	50	60	70	150	80	90
Total	50	60	70	260	80	90

He also estimates that employee headcount will increase substantially in Year 2 to staff the three plants, as is shown in Figure 7-16. Note the near quadrupling of employees outside of the United States and Canada over the two-year span from Year 0 to Year 2. Note also how revenues are projected to stagnate at about $230,000 per employee in Year 2 as the new employees ramp up to full productivity. We will introduce revenue projections for International Microwidgets in the next chapter.

Figure 7-16
International Microwidgets Employees at Year-End

Year	-2(A)	-1(A)	0(E)	1(F)	2(F)	3(F)
U.S./Canada	2600	2875	3240	3200	3200	3400
Rest of the World	300	325	360	600	1300	1500
Total Employees	**2900**	**3200**	**3600**	**3800**	**4500**	**4900**
Revenues/Employee ($000)	200	213	222	232	231	247

Figure 7-17 displays the historical and projected world-wide facility space of International Microwidgets. Note the transient increase in facility space per employee in Year 1 as the new plants are completed but the full complement of employees to staff them has not been reached.

Figure 7-17
International Microwidgets Facility Space at Year-End (Square feet)

Year	-2(A)	-1(A)	0(E)	1(F)	2(F)	3(F)
U.S./Canada	655	720	810	800	800	875
Rest of the World	70	80	90	310	325	350
Total Facility Space	**725**	**800**	**900**	**1110**	**1125**	**1225**
Facility Space/Employee	250	250	250	292	250	250

We will not go into the detail of Bill Portes's expense projection, but merely present the results. See Figure 7-18.

Figure 7-18
International Microwidgets Expenses ($ in millions)

Year	-2(A)	-1(A)	0(E)	1(F)	2(F)	3(F)
Marketing	145	170	200	220	255	300
Engineering	70	80	95	105	125	145
G&A	45	55	65	70	85	100
Total Expenses	**260**	**305**	**360**	**395**	**465**	**545**

SUMMARY

Here are the important things to remember about resource projections:

- The three categories of resources are people, facilities and equipment. All three categories of projections must ultimately be converted into dollars for inclusion into the financial projections.

- The fundamental unit of people projections is headcount. To convert headcount projections into expense projections, one must consider salaries or wage rates, overtime and shift premiums, bonuses and commissions, employee turnover and fringe benefits. A measure that is used to test the validity of headcount projections is revenue per employee.

- Facilities consist of land and buildings. The latter is frequently referred to as plant and is usually measured in square feet. A measure that is used to test the validity of plant projections is square feet per employee.

- Once converted into dollars, headcount projections flow directly to the operating statement as expenses.

- The flow of facilities and equipment projections to the financial projections depends on whether the company buys or leases the resources. If the company chooses to lease certain resources, the lease payment projections flow to the operating statement as expenses. Long-term lease obligations may also appear on the balance sheet.

- If the company chooses to purchase certain resources, those with a small dollar value or very short useful lives might be expensed, in which case their entire costs flow directly to the operating statement as items of expense.

- Normally, however, facilities and equipment that are purchased are capitalized. In this case, the costs of the purchases flow to the sources and uses of funds statement as uses of funds; the costs of the resources flow to the assets category of the balance sheet where they are reduced annually by depreciation; and the annual depreciation appears as an expense on the operating statement.

Projecting a company's forward resource needs is probably the most tedious element in the preparation of the strategic plan. My observation is that most planners err to one of two extremes when they attempt to forecast resources. Some treat the matter far too lightly and tend to underestimate the resources that will be required to implement the programs that they plan to undertake. The example of Industrial Terminal Systems in this chapter is a case in point.

Plans that underestimate future resource requirements usually look good on paper but are not even worth the paper that they are written on. Fortunately, such plans can usually be exposed for what they are by simple validity checks. Some of these validity tests have been covered in this chapter and still more will be covered in Chapter IX.

At the other extreme is the planner who approaches resource projections in detail comparable to that of an annual budget, which the financials of a strategic plan are not. Remember from Chapter II that the strategic plan lays the foundation for the annual operational plan for the ensuing year. The first-year resource projections in the strategic plan merely establish the general size and shape of the budget for that year. Detailed calculations and justifications should be saved for the budgeting process.

So, your challenge in forecasting your resource requirements is to not bog yourself down in detail as you would in preparing an annual budget, but still to develop projections that are rational and justifiable. Good luck in this section of your plan.

CHAPTER VIII

FINANCIAL PROJECTIONS

> Civilization and profits go hand in hand.
>
> Calvin Coolidge, 1920
>
> The trouble with the profit system has always been that it was highly unprofitable to most people.
>
> E.B. White, 1944

Discussed in this chapter is the last step in the preparation of the strategic business plan, the preparation of financial projections. To refresh your memory, Figure 8-1 is a replication of the graphic from Chapter II that depicts the flow of a strategic plan. In the preceding chapters, we have sequentially covered the following elements of a strategic plan:

- Mission (Chapter II): What is the purpose of our company? Why are we in business?

- Market (Chapter III): What is the size of the market that our company serves? How is it expected to change over the planning horizon, and why?

- Competition (Chapter IV): Who are our major competitors? What are their strengths and weaknesses? What shares of the market do they command? What strategies are they believed to be following?

- Self-Evaluation (Chapter V): What are our strengths and weaknesses? What is our market share?

- Opportunities and Threats (Chapter V): What opportunities exist upon which we can capitalize? What threats must be countered?

- Objectives (Chapter VI): What should we attempt to accomplish over the planning horizon?

- Strategies (Chapter VI): How do we intend to achieve these objectives?

- Programs (Chapter VI): What measurable activities will we undertake to implement these strategies?

- Goals (Chapter VI): By what specific quantitative measures will we track the progress of these programs?

- Resources (Chapter VII): What people, facilities, equipment and funds are required to carry out this plan?

In this final step, we will address such questions as:

- What revenues and profits can be expected to result from the strategic plan?

- How will funds be generated and used?

- What sort of balance sheets can be expected?

Figure 8-1
The Flow of a Strategic Plan

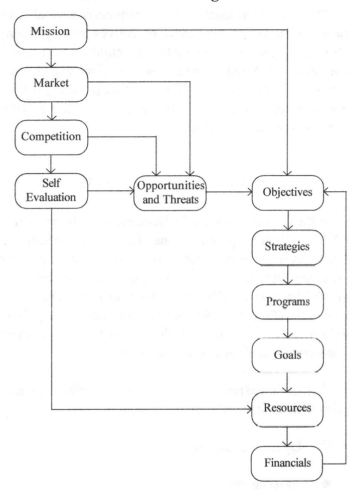

At this point in the planning process, ambition always runs
squarely into reality. This collision sends shock waves back
through much of the work that has been accomplished. It is
commonplace to find that revenue projections fall short of
expectations, that profit margins are less than satisfactory and
that the projected demand for resources exceeds reasonable

limits of availability.

The result is at least one and frequently several iterations back through the chain of objectives, strategies, programs and goals to reconcile the desirable with the practical. This is denoted by the arrow from Financials back to Objectives in Figure 8-1. The fact that planning is a dynamic process becomes readily apparent at this stage in the preparation of the plan.

FINANCIAL STATEMENTS

In the opening chapter, I discussed the hallmarks of an effective strategic planner. One of them was the ability to understand financial statements. This does not necessarily mean that an effective strategic planner be an MBA (which I am) or a CPA (which I am not). He must, however, have a fundamental understanding of accounting (however it was obtained), of the three basic types of financial statements, and of the interactions among them.

As mentioned previously, the three financial statements with which we are primarily concerned are the:

- Operating statement

- Balance sheet

- Sources and uses of funds.

These three statements are interdependent. Changes to one statement invariably result in changes to the other two. An example may help to convey the interlocking relationships among the statements.

Plan For Profitability!

Consider interest expense, which is a line item on the operating statement. Increased interest expense results in decreased net income on the operating statement. Thus, changes in interest expense result in changes to the operating statement.

The balance sheet will also change. Assume for this example that the increase in interest expense is caused by increased borrowing. In this case, liabilities on the balance sheet will increase to reflect the added debt, retained earnings will decrease because of the drop in net income, and the assets side of the balance sheet will increase to reflect the deployment of the added capital.

The funds flow statement will also change. The sources side of the statement will increase by the difference between the increased borrowing and the drop in net income. This difference will be reflected on the uses side according to how these additional funds are deployed.

Hence the question: where do we start? Consider for a moment the database that we have accumulated to this point in the development of the strategic plan. We have quantified the market that the company serves, both historical and projected. We know the company's historical market share and historical revenues. We have defined programs that will generate future revenues and have set goals to quantify the company's future revenue performance. Accordingly, we should be able to project a revenue stream for the company. Revenues are an element of the operating statement.

We have also quantified the resources that the company will require in the future to generate the projected revenues. The application of resources results in expense, which is also an element of the operating statement.

So, the logical place to start is with the operating statement. My preference is to start at the very top of the operating statement and work down to the bottom, interacting with the balance sheet as required in the process, such that the funds flow statement is essentially a mechanical result of the process. Starting with the operating statement is the most straightforward approach when one considers the database that we have constructed to this point.

REVENUE PROJECTIONS

For continuity, we shall continue with the example of ITS, which we introduced in the last chapter. This little company is one of the best examples that I have in my files. Its financials are straightforward and uncomplicated, yet they illustrate most of the salient principles in generating financial projections. Recall also that, for simplicity, we have shortened the time frame of the financial data to three years, the year in which the plan was generated (1985) and the next two years (1986-87).

The buildup of the revenue (and cost of revenue) calculations is illustrated in Figure 8-2. ITS had one model of computer terminal (the Model 10) in production at the time that these financial projections were generated in 1985 and expected to ship two additional models (Models 11 and 12) in mid-1986.

Plan For Profitability!

Figure 8-2
Revenue Projections

	1985(E)	1986(F)	1987(F)
Selling Price ($)			
Model 10	3,750	3,750	3,250
Model 11		5,000	4,500
Model 12		7,500	6,875
Cost of Goods Sold ($)			
Model 10	1,500	1,500	1,300
Model 11		2,500	2,250
Model 12		3,000	2,900
Sales (Units)			
Model 10	25	320	1,275
Model 11		35	265
Model 12		60	775
Operating Statement ($ in thousands except as noted)			
Sales Revenues	94	1,825	10,664
Cost of Goods Sold	38	748	4,501
Gross Profit	56	1,078	6,163
Gross Margin (%)	60%	59%	58%

As can be seen from the unit sales tabulation of Figure 8-2, ITS projected an extremely steep ramp in its shipments to revenue, growing from 25 terminals in 1985 to over 2300 terminals two year later. ITS reckoned that the latter figure still represented less than 5% of its served market. As is so often the case with start-up companies, ITS was not constrained so much by the size of its market as it was by its own ability to build the organizational structure to serve its market.

The average selling price of the company's terminals ranged from $3250 to $7500 per unit, these figures having been set to be competitive with the prices of competitors' products. Unit costs, derived from detailed cost buildups from the company's subcontract manufacturers, ranged from

$1300 to $3000 per unit. The average *gross margin* on the company's terminals was approximately 60%, where:

$$\text{Gross Margin} = \frac{\text{Selling Price - Cost}}{\text{Selling Price}}$$

Note also that ITS projected that the cost per unit would decline over time. For example, the cost of the Model 10 was projected to drop from $1500 in 1986 to $1300 in 1987. This is consistent with the principle of the learning curve that was discussed in Chapter V.

At the bottom of Figure 8-2 are the calculations which form the initial entries on the operating statement:

- Sales revenues, which increase from $94,000 in 1985 to $10,664,000 in 1987.

- Cost of goods sold: $38,000 in 1985, growing to $4,501,000 in 1987.

Note that the company's composite gross margin ranges from 58% to 60% over the period of the strategic plan. This figure is meaningful only when it is compared to the margins of the company's competitors (if their margins can be determined, for companies tend to guard product margin information zealously).

THE OPERATING STATEMENT

By now it should be apparent that a software spreadsheet program is an invaluable aid in managing the financial projections that are inherent to a strategic plan. From here on out, the use of a computer spreadsheet program is desirable. We have already made the point that changes to one financial statement invariably ripple through to the other two statements. Setting up interlocking spreadsheets ensures that an entry or a change to an entry on one statement will automatically be reflected on the other two statements.

Computer-based spreadsheets also ease the task of the inevitable iterations of the strategic plan and its financial projections. As mentioned previously, the first generation of the financial projections rarely results in an achievable scenario. Typically, profit projections fall short of expectations or expense projections are too high, or both. The planner then must shift to the mode of *what-if analysis*. For example, if a Marketing expense is reduced, what is the impact on revenues and profit? Or if R&D is increased, what is the effect? Interlocking software spreadsheets permit the planner to focus on the what-if without worrying about the mechanics of intra- and inter-spreadsheet dependencies.

I find it helpful to diagram these dependencies as a first step in setting up the spreadsheets on the computer. Most of my accounting friends don't need to resort to such a flow chart when they set up spreadsheets because the interdependencies are intrinsic to them. If you are in that category, you can skip this step. If not, Figure 8-3 is a roadmap of the principal interrelationships within the operating statement and the balance sheet for the ITS example. As we work down the operating statement, it may be helpful to refer to this roadmap.

FIGURE 8-3
OPERATING STATEMENT-BALANCE SHEET
INTERACTIONS

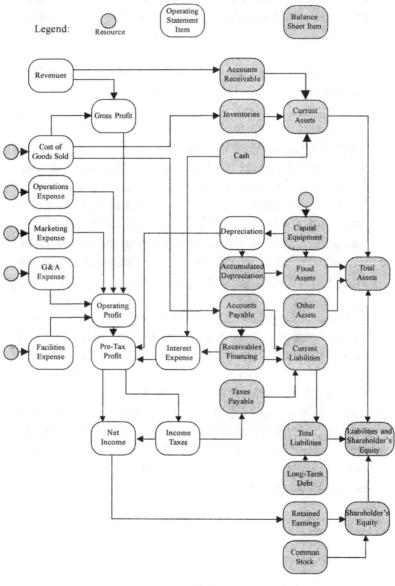

Plan For Profitability!

Figure 8-4 is the operating statement, the first line of which is *revenues*. These flow directly from the company's projections of market share and resulting revenues. In the case of ITS, revenues flow from the projections of Figure 8-2.

Figure 8-4
The Operating Statement
($ in thousands, except as noted)

	1985(E)	1986(F)	1987(F)
Revenues	94	1,826	10,664
Cost of Goods Sold	38	748	4,501
Gross Profit	56	1,078	6,163
Marketing	39	543	1,688
Operations	202	321	933
General & Administrative	143	253	415
Facilities	12	45	90
Total Expenses	396	1,162	3,125
Operating Profit	(340)	(84)	3,038
Depreciation	4	34	66
Interest	85	105	209
	89	139	275
Pre-Tax Profit	(429)	(223)	2,763
Income Taxes	-	-	550
Net Income	(429)	(223)	2,213
Return on Sales (%)	-457%	-12%	21%
Earnings per Share ($)	-0.36	-0.19	1.84
Shares Outstanding	1,200	1,200	1,200

(thousands)

Cost of goods sold is also transferred from Figure 8-2 and becomes the second line of the operating statement of Figure 8-4. Cost of goods sold is derived from detailed projections of the cost of manufacturing each of the products in the product forecast. Key considerations in calculating cost of goods sold include:

- Manufacturing labor costs, both direct and indirect. These should flow directly from and correlate with the manufacturing headcount projections. In the case of ITS, manufacturing headcount was not significant because of the decision to subcontract manufacturing.

- Material costs.

- Manufacturing plant and equipment overhead, which, as with labor, should tie in with the resource projections.

- Labor and material inflation assumptions. We discussed inflation in Chapter III.

- Improvements in manufacturing efficiency. To reiterate, an important tool in this regard is the learning curve.

On the operating statement, *gross profit* is the difference between revenues and cost of goods sold. We introduced the concept of *gross margin* in the last chapter. It is defined as:

$$\text{Gross Margin} = \frac{\text{Gross Profit}}{\text{Revenues}}$$

Gross margin is one of the most important measurements of the inherent profitability of the business. We will expand upon this in a subsequent chapter.

The next group of expenses on the operating statement is non-manufacturing in nature, viz., *Marketing, Operations* (primarily Engineering for ITS, since the company planned to subcontract its manufacturing), and *General and Administrative*. The latter expense category encompasses those costs that are not included in the first two categories and typically includes Finance, Legal, Human Resources, the Chief Executive Officer, the Chief Operating Officer and, oh yes, Strategic Planning. (Of course, ITS was too small to afford all of these functions.) These expenses also flow directly from the resource projections in the form of headcount costs. In the case of ITS, these projections were developed in the last chapter and can be found in Figure 7-12.

Facilities expense is also derived from the resource calculations, specifically the plant (floor space) projections. We developed the ITS facilities projections in the preceding chapter and they are summarized in Figure 7-13.

Generally, facilities expense is allocated among the components of the organization in proportion to their occupancy and use of the facilities. As a result, facilities expense does not usually appear as a separate line item on the operating statement, but rather is distributed as an overhead factor to Manufacturing, Engineering, Marketing, Sales, Finance, etc. Since ITS was so small, however, its management decided to show facilities expense as a single line item on the P&L statement rather than apportion it as would have been the normal procedure.

The company's decision to lease its facilities (which is common for start-up companies) resulted in the entire cost of the facilities being written off on the operating statement.

Had ITS purchased its facilities, only the depreciation component of the facilities would have appeared on the operating statement.

Operating profit follows as the next line on the operating statement of Figure 8-4. Operating profit measures the operational profitability of the business, i.e., profitability prior to depreciation, interest and tax charges.

Depreciation is also derived from the capital equipment section of the resource calculations, specifically from Figure 7-14 in the case of ITS. Like facilities expense, depreciation is usually allocated among the components of the organization and does not generally appear as a line item on the P&L statement.

The next line of the operating statement, *interest expense*, is an item that is driven by the balance sheet. You may wish to refer to the roadmap of Figure 8-3 to see the interaction. Accordingly, it is time to introduce the balance sheet for ITS, Figure 8-5.

Interest income on the operating statement is produced by cash (and cash equivalents) on the balance sheet, while current and long-term debt on the balance sheet generates interest expense on the operating statement. This calculation is fairly straightforward and hinges on the analyst's forecast of interest rates over the planning period.

In the case of ITS, the company was strapped for cash, so that interest income from cash and cash equivalents was negligible. With regard to interest expense, the company had two credit arrangements at the time these projections were made. They were:

1) An $840,000 note from a shareholder. The terms of this note stipulated simple interest at 10% ($84,000) per year, with both principal and interest due in a balloon payment at the end of 1987.

2) A line of credit from the company's bank, the amount of which was tied to the company's outstanding receivables. The arrangement provided that the bank would grant the company a floating line of credit (see *receivables financing* in Figure 8-5) equal to two-thirds of the face value of its accounts receivable and that the rate of interest would be 14% per annum, payable quarterly, over the two-year forecast period.

Both the interest on the $840,000 note and on the bank line of credit appear on the operating statement as interest expense. For example, in 1987, the total interest expense was projected to be $209,000, as shown in Figure 8-4. Since the annual interest on the note was fixed at $84,000, the difference of $125,000 represents the projected interest expense on the bank loan. We shall discuss how the bank loan interest was derived shortly.

The next line on the operating statement (Figure 8-4), *pretax profit*, consists of operating profit less depreciation and interest expense. This, in turn, leads to the next line of the operating statement, *income taxes*. These consist of local, state, federal and foreign levies, with federal taxes usually constituting the bulk of the total.

Figure 8-5
The Balance Sheet
(Year End)
($ in thousands)

	1985(E)	1986(F)	1987(F)
Cash	109	(494)	337
Accounts Receivable	24	457	2,666
Inventories	38	299	1,800
Current Assets	171	262	4,803
Capital Equipment	20	172	329
Less: Accumulated Depreciation	4	38	104
Fixed Assets	16	134	225
Start-Up Costs	62	62	62
Other Assets	62	62	62
Total Assets	**249**	**458**	**5,090**
Accounts Payable	3	62	375
Receivables Financing	16	35	1,777
Taxes Payable	-	-	550
Current Liabilities	19	367	2,702
Deferred Interest	168	252	336
Shareholder Note	840	840	840
Long-Term Debt	1,008	1,092	1,176
Total Liabilities	**1,027**	**1,459**	**3,878**
Common Stock	212	212	212
Retained Earnings (Deficit)	(990)	(1,213)	1,000
Shareholder's Equity	(778)	(1,001)	1,212
Total Liabilities & Equity	**249**	**458**	**5,090**

Plan For Profitability!

At the time of this plan, federal corporate taxes were capped at 46% of pre-tax income, but most companies paid less than this maximum rate due to tax credits, such as credits for investment in property and equipment and in research and development or by manufacturing at foreign sites that had more favorable tax rates than the United States. The projection of income taxes over the planning horizon is a function of the company's deployment of its resources, and well managed companies always attempt to minimize taxes as one of the considerations in resource deployment.

Start-up companies like ITS, however, are generally so capital-constrained that they cannot take advantage of the tax incentives suggested in the prior paragraph. Fortunately, start-ups frequently have an even better tax advantage, net operating loss (NOL) carryforward, which is simply prior period losses that can be applied to offset pre-tax income in future periods prior to the calculation of income taxes.

ITS had accumulated $561,000 of NOL carryforward through 1984. Moreover, from Figure 8-4, it can be seen that the company projected that it would continue to lose $429,000 in 1985 and another $223,000 in 1986, such that it would have accumulated a total NOL carryforward of $1,213,000 upon entering into its first profitable year, 1987. In other words, in 1987 the company's first $1,213,000 of profit would be tax-free, since the NOL carryforward would offset the taxable income. The net effect was that ITS projected that its tax burden in 1987 would be low, viz., only $550,000 on $2,763,000 of income, which is only 19%.

The bottom line of the operating statement is, of course, *net income*. Note that ITS projected two more years of loss, the year in which the plan was prepared and the year thereafter, before turning profitable in 1987.

One of the measures of the profit performance of a company is *return on sales* (ROS), which is simply:

$$ROS = \frac{\text{Net Income}}{\text{Revenues}}$$

The ROS's of well-managed manufacturing companies typically fall in the range of 4-10%, depending on the industry. Note that ITS projected that it would achieve an ROS of 21% in its first year of profitability. Needless to say, this figure met with some skepticism.

A figure that securities analysts follow closely is *earnings per share* (EPS):

$$EPS = \frac{\text{Net Income}}{\text{Shares Outstanding}}$$

For publicly traded companies, EPS is a major determinant the price of a company's shares. Note the EPS calculations for ITS at the bottom of the operating statement.

You may recall that, at the outset of the ITS example, we mentioned that ITS was seeking *equity capital* in the amount of $2 million. In other words, ITS was prepared to issue additional shares to investors in exchange for $2 million. These additional shares that were proposed to be issued to a new venture capital investor were not included in the operating statement projections of Figure 8-4. This exclusion was intentional on the part of ITS, for it avoided the company's concern of prematurely valuing the new shares (and perhaps undervaluing them). Likewise, the infusion of $2 million of equity capital was not shown as a source of funds on the funds flow statement, nor did it appear on the balance sheet. The issuance of these new shares would, of course, cause the projected EPS to be lower than shown in Figure 8-4 according to the amount of additional shares issued.

THE BALANCE SHEET

Figure 8-5 is the balance sheet for ITS. As we proceed through the balance sheet, you may wish to continue to refer to Figure 8-3 and its roadmap of the interplay between the balance sheet and the operating statement.

The line item on the balance sheet which is the last to be filled in is either *cash* (and cash equivalents) or *debt* (both long-term and current). These entries may be viewed as *plugs* to make the balance sheet balance. In the example of the ITS balance sheet, cash is the plug so that we can ascertain the amount of funding that the company requires. Cash is permitted to go negative, which is an unrealistic situation, of course. See the first line of Figure 8-5.

Balance sheet projections are more creative than those of the operating statement. Assumptions must be made about the financial efficiency with which the company will be run over the planning horizon. In my experience, the tendency is to predict more efficient performance than has been achieved in the past, and more often than not the result is precisely the contrary.

This unrealistic optimism is particularly prevalent in companies that predict rapid growth, such as ITS. CEO's of such companies often underestimate the challenge of orchestrating the growth alone, let alone improving operating efficiencies at the same time. But I have jumped into considerations about the validity of the strategic plan, which are covered in a later chapter.

An example may help to illustrate my point. To minimize demands for working capital, companies try to collect their accounts receivable as quickly as possible and defer remitting their accounts payable for as long as they can. The catch is that all of the companies with which a company deals are striving to accomplish the same thing. Suppliers (accounts payable) are pressuring the company for payment, while customers (accounts receivable) stretch out payments. My experience is that the best gauge of efficiency in future payments and collections is a company's past performance. However, since ITS is a start-up, there is no past performance on which we can base the future. This is where creativity comes into play.

Proceed to the second line of the balance sheet, *accounts receivable*. The roadmap of Figure 8-3 shows that receivables are a function of revenues (from the operating statement). The relationship is essentially a direct one: as revenues increase, so usually do accounts receivable. The coefficient that ties these two variables together is *days receivables*, which is a measure of the age of the average receivable when it is paid. Days receivables is derived as follows:

Days Receivables = 365 x <u>Accounts Receivable</u>
Annual Revenues

In ITS's projections, the company assumed 90 days aging of its receivables, a reasonably conservative estimate. In other words, the company assumed its invoices would be collected, on the average, 90 days after they were generated. By rearranging the above equation, we can see that revenues (from the operating statement) determine accounts receivable (on the balance sheet) as follows:

$$\text{Accounts Receivable} = \frac{90}{365} \times \text{Revenues}$$

In short, accounts receivable were assumed to amount to approximately one-quarter of the revenues for the year. Take, for example, the year 1986, in which revenues (from the operating statement) were projected to amount to $1,825,000. Accounts receivable at the end of 1986 (from the balance sheet) amount to $457,000, which is one-quarter of revenues.

Next on the balance sheet are *inventories*, which are dependent upon the cumulative flow of manufactured product on the operating statement, which is reflected in cost of goods sold. The accepted measure of inventory efficiency is annual *inventory turns*, i.e., how many times the inventory is cycled each year. This can be calculated according to the following expression:

$$\text{Inventory Turns} = \frac{\text{Cost of Goods Sold}}{\text{Inventories}}$$

ITS assumed that it could turn its inventories 2.5 times per year, which was a conservative projection since the company subcontracted its manufacturing and ostensibly could strive for *just-in-time* control of inventory. Nonetheless, ITS assumed that, at any point in time, the value of goods on hand in inventory was equivalent to the cost of goods to be sold in four-tenths (1 / 2.5) of a year:

$$\text{Inventories} = \frac{4}{10} \times \text{Cost of Goods Sold}$$

To test this calculation, note that cost of goods sold in 1987 (from Figure 8-4) is about $4.5 million. Four-tenths of this amount is $1.8 million, which is the value of inventories at the end of 1987 (from Figure 8-5).

Back to Figure 8-5, cash (which has not yet been filled in at this point in our buildup of the balance sheet), accounts receivable and inventories sum to form *current assets*. The next item on the balance sheet, *capital equipment*, flows directly from the resource projections (Figure 7-14).

Each depreciable asset that is added to the company's asset listing must, of course, be depreciated over its useful life span. See Figure 7-14 for the depreciation component of ITS's capital equipment. The sum of the depreciation schedules for new and existing equipment results in *accumulated depreciation* on the balance sheet. The difference between the acquisition value of the fixed assets and accumulated depreciation is *net fixed assets*.

The category of *other assets* on the balance sheet contains items that are specific to the history of the company. In the case of ITS, the company elected to capitalize its early start-up costs of $62,000. The sum of current assets, fixed assets and other assets yields *total assets*. This completes the assets side of the balance sheet.

On the liabilities side of the balance sheet, let us first consider *accounts payable*, which, like inventories and receivables, are driven by the operating statement. Since companies usually pay their employees promptly, the bulk of accounts payable are due to outsiders and are referred to as *trade payables*. Although some of these trade payables are for non-manufacturing expenses, most of them are related to manufacturing, specifically to cost of goods sold. Thus, it is possible to derive a coarse measure of the efficiency with which a company pays its bills (or, more aptly, the inefficiency, since it is desirable to delay payment as long as possible and realize the de facto use of the cash). This measure, *days payables*, is derived as follows:

$$\text{Days Payables} = 365 \times \frac{\text{Accounts Payable}}{\text{Cost of Goods Sold}}$$

For ITS this figure was assumed to be 30 days, a conservative figure that connotes very prompt payment of receivables. Since 30/365 is approximately one-twelfth, accounts payable (on the balance sheet) were determined by cost of goods sold (on the operating statement) as follows:

$$\text{Accounts Payable} = \frac{1}{12} \times \text{Cost of Goods Sold}$$

To the line labeled *receivables financing* on the balance sheet (Figure 8-5), I mentioned earlier that ITS had an arrangement for a line of credit with its bank equal to two-thirds of the face value of its accounts receivable. In 1987, note that the liability of receivables financing of $1,777,000 is two-thirds of accounts receivable of $2,666,000. Recall also that the rate of interest on this line of credit was 14% per annum, payable quarterly. Quarterly calculations (not shown) determined the annual interest in 1987 to be $125,000, which, combined with the interest on the shareholder's loan of $84,000, amount to $209,000, the amount of interest expense on the operating statement of Figure 8-4.

The next item on the balance sheet is *taxes payable*. These flow directly from the line entitled *income taxes* on the operating statement. As shown on the flow chart, accounts payables, receivables financing and taxes payable combine to form *current liabilities*.

Long-term debt for ITS consisted of the $840,000 note and the interest accrued upon it (*deferred interest*). The sum of current liabilities and long-term debt forms *total liabilities* and finishes the liabilities side of the balance sheet. You will recall that cash on the assets side of the balance sheet has not been filled in at this juncture.

Shareholders' equity consists of two components: *common stock* and *retained earnings*. The latter flows directly from net income after cash dividends. Since ITS had not paid and did not plan to pay any cash dividends, the entirety of each year's net income flows to increase retained earnings.

This brings us to the common stock line of the balance sheet (Figure 8-5) and the paramount consideration of how the company will be capitalized over the planning period. *Simply put, a business generates its capital needs in two ways: internally from operations, or externally via the assumption of debt or the issuance of equity.*

With regard to the equity alternative, I prefer not to project equity offerings over the planning horizon. The trade-off of debt versus equity is one that should be made at the time the external capital is required, taking into account the relative receptivity of the securities market to bonds versus stock and the relative costs of the two alternatives.

For the sake of the financial projections of the strategic plan, it is more straightforward and predictable to assume that external capital is generated by debt, which only requires that the planner project future interest rates. The equity alternative demands that he predict the price-to-earnings multiple that the company's stock will command at some future date. I personally prefer not to attempt such crystal ball gazing.

The completion of the balance sheet from here on out is essentially a mechanical process. Additional debt needs to be assumed in a given forecast year if a deficit cash position results without the debt. If cash is positive, then no new debt is required. If cash is in substantial surplus, then some of the prior debt can be retired.

In the balance sheet of Figure 8-5, we have taken a slightly different tack. Consistent with the foregoing philosophy, we did not forecast the equity issue for the simple reason that ITS preferred to let the market determine the number of shares the company would have to issue to receive its needed capital. However, the alternative of additional debt was not a reasonable one, since the company, with over $1 million of liabilities at the end of 1985, could not obtain more credit. So, with the cash line as the plug, we merely let the cash line go negative to that amount which balances the balance sheet.

So, based on the financials of their strategic plan, how much capital did ITS need? Clearly, the company needed enough to cover the deficit cash position, which was projected to peak at $494,000 at year-end 1986. So, at a minimum, ITS needed this amount. On the other hand, ITS projected that it would generate cash in 1987, as witnessed by the positive cash position of $337,000 at the end of 1987. The equity capital of $494,000 used in 1986 would be more than restored in 1987.

The company was also required to pay off the note to its shareholder with accrued interest at the end of 1987, which was projected to be (from Figure 8-5) $1,176,000. The company also had to pay its income taxes in early 1988 in the amount of $550,000. Combined, these two amounted to $1,726,000. With a reserve for additional working capital, ITS framed its request to the venture capital community at $2 million.

Upon obtaining the capital, the *shareholders' equity* section of the balance sheet should be increased by the amount of the equity capital, long-term debt should be retired, and cash should be increased to bring the line to positive figures. EPS on the operating statement should decrease, of course, because of the additional shares outstanding.

THE FUNDS FLOW STATEMENT

Figure 8-6 is the statement of sources and uses of funds. It follows directly from the operating statement and the balance sheet.

INTERNATIONAL MICROWIDGETS

Figure 8-7 displays six years of historical and projected operating statements for International Microwidgets. The revenue projections are derived from detailed forecasts (not shown) of revenues in each of the six regions of the world. Projected revenues do not include those from the acquisition of General Microwidgets, which is treated as an adjunct to the strategic plan. This is discussed in Chapter XI.

Plan For Profitability!

Figure 8-6
The Funds Flow Statement
($ in millions)

	1985(E)	1986(F)	1987(F)
Cash at Beginning of Year	404	109	(494)
Sources of Cash			
Net Income (Loss)	(429)	(223)	2,213
Depreciation	4	34	66
Accounts Payable	3	59	313
Receivables Financing	16	289	1,472
Deferred Interest	84	84	84
Deferred Taxes	-	-	550
Total Sources	(332)	243	4,698
Uses of Cash			
Accounts Receivable	24	433	2,209
Inventories	38	261	1,501
Capital Equipment	20	152	157
Total Uses	82	846	3,867
Cash at End of Year	109	(494)	337

Projections for cost of revenues reflect internal manufacture of semiconductor chips and the addition of assembly plants in China and Eastern Europe, both of which occur at the end of Year 1. Note the steady decline in gross margin from 60% in Year -2 to 57% in Year 1, which statistically confirms the weakness of declining product margins. With internal chip sourcing and lower cost assembly plants on line for Years 2 and 3 of the plan, Bill Portes projects that margins will recover robustly in the final two years of the plan.

Figure 8-7
International Microwidgets Operating Statement
($ in millions)

Year	-2(A)	-1(A)	0(E)	1(F)	2(F)	3(F)
Revenues	580	680	800	880	1040	1210
Cost of Revenues	230	180	340	380	430	470
Gross Profit	**350**	**400**	**460**	**500**	**610**	**740**
Gross Margin	60%	59%	58%	57%	59%	61%
Marketing	145	170	200	220	255	300
Engineering	70	80	95	105	125	145
General and						
Administrative	45	55	65	70	85	100
Total Expenses	**260**	**305**	**360**	**395**	**465**	**545**
Operating Profit	**90**	**95**	**100**	**105**	**145**	**195**
Interest	0	0	0	16	15	14
Depreciation	30	35	40	45	50	60
Interest &						
Depreciation	**30**	**35**	**40**	**61**	**65**	**75**
Pre-Tax Income	**60**	**60**	**60**	**44**	**80**	**121**
Taxes	20	20	20	15	30	45
Net Income	**40**	**40**	**40**	**29**	**50**	**76**
Net Income/						
Revenue	7%	6%	5%	3%	5%	6%
Earning Per Share(s)	2.31	2.30	2.29	1.65	2.81	4.25

Marketing, Engineering, and General and Administrative expenses flow directly from the resource projections. Note that operating profit (gross profit less expenses) increases sparsely from Year -2 through Year 1, as declining gross margin neutralizes the vigorous growth in revenues. When margins turn around, however, operating profit takes off, nearly doubling over the final two years of the plan.

Interest and depreciation expenses are derived from the balance sheet, Figure 8-8. In its recent history, the company has been able to operate without any debt. As many technology companies do, International Microwidgets has abstained from paying dividends to its shareholders, and its earnings have been sufficient to fund the growth of the company.

Figure 8-8
International Microwidgets Balance Sheet
($ in millions)

Year	-2(A)	-1(A)	0(E)	1(F)	2(F)	3(F)
Cash and Equivalents	115	110	94	94	71	75
Accounts Receivable	97	113	133	147	173	202
Inventory	193	227	267	293	347	403
Current Assets	**405**	**450**	**494**	**534**	**591**	**680**
Property, Plant and Equipment	600	660	730	990	1070	1160
Less Accumulated Depreciation	400	435	475	520	570	630
Fixed Assets	**200**	**225**	**255**	**470**	**500**	**530**
Total Assets	**605**	**675**	**749**	**1004**	**1091**	**1210**
Accounts Payable	116	136	160	176	208	242
Current Portion of Long-Term Debt	0	0	0	10	10	10
Taxes Payable	5	5	5	5	10	15
Current Liabilities	**121**	**141**	**165**	**191**	**228**	**267**
Long-Term Debt	**0**	**0**	**0**	**190**	**180**	**170**
Total Liabilities	**121**	**141**	**165**	**381**	**408**	**437**
Paid-In Capital	100	105	110	115	120	125
Retained Earnings	500	540	580	620	649	699
Shareholders' Equity	**600**	**645**	**690**	**735**	**769**	**824**
Total Liabilities and Equity	**721**	**786**	**855**	**1116**	**1177**	**1261**
Outstanding Shares (millions)	17.3	17.4	17.5	17.6	17.7	17.8

To fund the new plants, however, Portes plans to borrow $200 million at a competitive rate (8%) and to retire the debt at a conservative pace of $10 million per year. The interest on this debt in Year 1 ($16 million) will clearly sock an already bleak earnings forecast. Note that net income, which has been stagnant at $40 million per year for three years, is projected to drop to $29 million in Year 1 due to the impact of the interest on the debt. Likewise, earnings per share are forecast to tumble from a three-year plateau of $2.30 to $1.65.

We will explore the trade-off between debt and equity financing and the topic of dilution in more detail in Chapter XI. For the time being, here is an abbreviated version of the analysis of the issue by Bill Portes. At the time he is working on these financial projections, shares of International Microwidgets are trading at $46 and there are 17.5 million shares outstanding. With per-share earnings of $2.30, shares of International Microwidgets are trading at a price-to-earnings multiple of 20x.

At first glance, it would appear that raising $200 million in equity financing requires the issuance of 4.35 million new shares ($200 million ÷ $46). However, that volume of new shares on the market will surely depress the price of the stock. Assuming that the P/E multiple will hold at 20x with the addition of the new shares, Portes calculates that the share price would fall to $34. This would necessitate the issuance of 5.9 million additional shares to raise $200 million, bringing the total outstanding shares to 23.4 million.

With net income of $40 million, earnings per share in Year 1 under this equity scenario would be $1.71 ($40 million ÷ 23.4 million shares), which is slightly higher than the forecast of $1.65 under the debt scenario. However, Portes is reluctant to flood the market with such a large secondary offering, especially since he plans to issue new shares for the acquisition of General Microwidgets. Accordingly, he opts for debt to fund the new plants.

Note that, although the plant expansion program effects a significant drop in net income and earning per share in Year 1, both recover soundly in Years 2 and 3. By the final year of the plan, earnings are almost twice the level of the three-year plateau from Year -2 to Year 0.

Figure 8-9 is the funds flow statement for International Microwidgets.

SUMMARY

Chapter VIII has covered the final element of the strategic plan, financial statements. Among the points to be retained in this chapter are the following:

- The preparation of financial statements marks that point in the preparation of the strategic plan where ambition and reality confront one another. The compromises that result necessitate that earlier parts of the plan be reworked.

- The three key financial statements are the operating statement, the balance sheet and the funds flow statement. My preference is to begin with the operating statement and complete it in concert with the balance sheet.

- If external working capital is indicated over the planning horizon, it is more conservative to assume that the capital will be raised via debt than by equity. Then, the trade-off of debt versus equity can be made at the time the capital is needed in the light of then-current securities market conditions.

Figure 8-9
International Microwidgets Funds Flow Statement
($ in millions)

Year	-2(A)	-1(A)	0(E)	1(F)	2(F)	3(F)
Cash at						
Beginning of Year	125	115	110	94	94	71
Sources of Cash						
Net Income	40	40	40	29	50	76
Depreciation	30	35	40	45	50	60
Accounts Payable	15	20	24	16	32	34
Deferred Taxes	5	5	5	5	10	15
Paid-In Capital	5	5	5	5	5	5
Long-Term Debt	0	0	0	200	0	0
Total Sources	**95**	**105**	**114**	**300**	**147**	**190**
Uses of Cash						
Accounts Receivable	15	17	20	13	27	28
Inventory	40	33	40	27	53	57
Property, Plant & Equipment	50	60	70	260	80	90
Repayment of Debt	0	0	0	0	10	10
Total Uses	**105**	**110**	**130**	**300**	**170**	**185**
Cash at End						
of Year	**115**	**110**	**94**	**94**	**71**	**75**

CHAPTER IX
EVALUATING THE PLAN

In the end, you're measured not by how much you undertake but by what you finally accomplish.
Donald Trump, *The Art of the Deal*, 1987

The reward of a thing well done is to have done it.
Ralph Waldo Emerson, 1844

George Steiner writes that strategic planning "deals with the futurity of current decisions."[1] The ultimate test of the perception of a strategic plan occurs well out in the planning horizon, usually in its second half, when the management of the company must live with the results, good or bad, of its past decisions. Moreover, the results themselves form an integral part of the company's then current environment and represent part of the foundation for the company's strategic plan at that time.

Hence, the rational person might ask: can one test the validity of a strategic plan at its creation, rather than have to wait through much of the period covered by the plan? In fact, there are certain indicators to look for and examine, and we shall cover them in this chapter. However, a strategic plan is somewhat like a time bomb. Its ultimate test comes when it finally detonates. Unfortunately, there is no opportunity then to correct mistakes.

---

[1] George A. Steiner, Strategic Planning, The Free Press, New York, 1979

Before we proceed to the topic of testing the strategic plan, let me dwell for a moment on a common misconception about strategic plans. Many people are under the impression that once a strategic plan is published, it is inviolate. This misconception is particularly prevalent among middle managers, some of whom believe that a strategic plan is akin to a set of stone tablets that are the CEO's commandments until new tablets are issued at the same time next year.

To the contrary, in the real world, an SBU's environment is hardly so accommodating as to change annually and in coincidence with the preparation of the SBU's next strategic plan. As significant environmental changes occur during the course of the year between plans, the CEO and his staff should evaluate them and, if necessary, modify the plan. I do not advocate republishing the plan unless the changes are massive. All that is required is that the substance of the changes be communicated to those who need to know.

Although the strategic plan changes from year to year, my experience is that the changes are more evolutionary than revolutionary. A set of several years' strategic plans (of which I have several in my archives) brings to mind the ritual photograph of the gathering at an annual family reunion. From year to year there are changes in the photographs. Family members age, new faces appear, other faces drop from the scene, seating priorities change, but, taken in the context of the whole, the changes are gradual. So also is it usually with year-to-year strategic plans for an SBU.

Once the strategic plan is completed, there are sundry tests that can be applied to evaluate the plan. These are referred to as *validity tests* or *sanity checks*, which are expressions for common business sense. The most prevalent of such tests involve examining key statistics and their trends and spotting unrealistic or optimistic expectations.

This brings me to an observation that I have made so much among my colleagues that they refer to it as *Hargrave's Law.* It holds that an unfavorable trend will continue unabated unless positive action is taken to stop it and that positive action is also required to sustain a favorable trend. We shall see several examples of Hargrave's Law in action in this chapter.

GROSS MARGIN

When I look at a set of financial projections, one of the first checks I make is that of *gross margin (GM).* You will recall from Chapter VII that:

$$\text{Gross Margin} = \frac{\text{Gross Profit}}{\text{Revenues}}$$

The check is for gross margin is for both its trend and its value relative to the gross margins of the SBU's competitors. A declining gross margin trend can be symptomatic of manufacturing inefficiencies, unrealistic pricing, or both. An even worse situation is when the SBU's gross margin is lower than those of its competitors. The learning curve principle would suggest that the cause of this inequity lies in the SBU's lower cumulative volume and production experience, but there can be other causes as well.

RETURN MEASUREMENTS

In modern jargon, the "bottom line" refers to the most important and final consideration of the subject at hand. The expression derives from the bottom line of the operating statement, net income, which is the most important single parameter by which a company is measured. In this section, we will examine measures that are derived from net income and are termed *return measurements*.

Return on sales (ROS) was introduced in the preceding chapter. ROS compares the bottom line (net income) with the top line (revenues). The term ROS is actually a misnomer, since many companies derive revenues by means other than sales, such as by rentals, leases, etc. Nonetheless, ROS is the accepted terminology and is derived as follows:

$$ROS = \frac{Net\ Income}{Revenues}$$

ROS and gross margin are tightly interrelated. The go-between is *discretionary expenses*. Discretionary expenses encompass Marketing, Engineering, and G&A, all burdened by facilities and depreciation allocations. These expense are viewed as discretionary because the company has some latitude about how much or how little resources to apply to these categories of expense.

On a simplistic basis, the operating statement may be viewed as having four components of expense from the top line to the bottom line: cost of goods sold, discretionary expenses, interest and taxes. In other words, a rudimentary operating statement looks like this:

Plan For Profitability!

Revenues	100%
- Cost of Goods Sold	
Gross Profit	GM (%)
- Discretionary Expenses	
Operating Profit	
- Interest	
Pre-Tax Profit	
- Income Taxes	
Net Income	ROS (%)

For most strategic plans, a company's marginal tax rate (i.e., its income taxes as a percentage of pre-tax profit) is relatively constant over the planning horizon. Likewise, unless the company makes a significant change to its debt structure during the period of the plan, interest expenses may be viewed as relatively fixed. If you will permit me to take a little latitude with the foregoing simplified operating statement and simplify it even more to make my point:

Revenues	
- Cost of Goods Sold	
Gross Profit	Gross Margin
- Discretionary Expenses	
Operating Profit	
- Interest and Taxes	Fixed (to a first approximation)
Net Income	ROS

This illustrates that discretionary expenses are the link between gross margin and ROS. If the gross margin of an SBU deteriorates, the only way to keep ROS from deteriorating too is to trim discretionary expenses.

Looking at it another way, given two businesses with equal ROS's, the business with the higher gross margin will have more funds to devote to discretionary expenses. Plowing additional funds into Marketing and Engineering, if it is done wisely, should fuel additional revenue growth and profitability.

219

As the lyrics of the song *Ain't We Got Fun* go, "the rich get rich and the poor get poorer."

In 1984, I reviewed the strategic plan of NBI, a Colorado-based public company engaged in the market for office automation systems and supplies. Figure 9-1 displays several return measurements for the company over the nine years of its strategic plan (1981-89).

Figure 9-1
Return Measurements

	1981(A)	1982(A)	1983(A)	1984(E)	1985(F)	1986(F)	1987(F)	1988(F)	1989(F)
ROS	12.5%	11.0%	3.7%	4.7%	4.8%	4.3%	4.2%	6.0%	6.1%
ROE	15.8%	14.0%	5.2%	8.8%	9.7%	9.7%	11.8%	20.0%	20.8%
ROI	15.6%	13.9%	3.4%	6.1%	7.2%	5.9%	7.2%	12.4%	14.0%
EPS	$ 0.81	$ 1.18	$ 0.45	$ 0.82	$1.01	$1.10	$1.01	$3.18	$4.07

The data of Figure 9-1 shows that ROS dropped in 1983 (the year prior to that in which the plan was prepared) to 3.7%, was projected to stay in a band between 4% and 5% through 1987, after which it was forecast to jump to 6%. In assessing this ROS history and projections, two questions jump out of the nine-year stream of ROS data and beg to be answered:

   1) What caused the precipitous drop in ROS from 11% in 1982 to 3.7% in 1983?

   2) Is it reasonable to forecast a jump of 1.8 points in ROS in 1988? If so, why?

Keep these two questions in mind. We will develop the tools and skills to answer both of them before this chapter is over.

Plan For Profitability!

A second measure of return, also tabulated in Figure 9-1, is *return on shareholders' equity (ROE)*, given by:

$$ROE = \frac{Net\ Income}{Equity}$$

ROE is a measure of the company's return relative to the shareholders' paid-in capital and subsequent retained earnings. Examination of the ROE line of Figure 9-1 reveals a pattern similar to that for ROS, viz., a sharp drop in 1983 and a sharp increase in 1988, thus prompting two questions for ROE comparable to the two just asked for ROS.

Return on investment (ROI) is a measure of the company's return on the total capital employed in the enterprise, both equity and debt, and is defined as follows:

$$ROI = \frac{Net\ Income}{Equity + Debt}$$

Note that in years 1981 and 1982, ROI was approximately equal to ROE. This stems from the fact that the company had negligible debt during those two years. Thereafter, ROI tracks from 1.9 to 7.6 points below ROE, which implies that the company acquired debt in 1983 and planned to retain debt through the end of the planning period.

The measure of return that is most important to a company's shareholders is *earnings per share (EPS)*:

$$EPS = \frac{Net\ Income}{Shares\ Outstanding}$$

Steady growth in annual EPS usually results in appreciation of the market value of the company's shares. The *price-*

to-earnings multiple (P/E) is the ratio between the price of the company's stock and EPS:

$$P/E = \frac{\text{Share Price}}{\text{EPS}}$$

Thus, if one dares to attempt to predict the forward behavior of a company's P/E, the forecast of EPS in the company's strategic plan can be translated into a forecast of the price of the company's shares. This is one of the reasons that companies guard the confidentiality of their strategic plans. Disclosure of the plans to the public could be viewed as the company's best estimate of the future price of its shares.

See Figure 9-1 for the EPS of our company. In mid-1984, when the strategic plan had just been completed, the company's stock was selling at $6.00 per share. The most recent annual information available to the public (for year-end 1983) disclosed that the company had earned $0.45 per share. On this basis, the stock was trading at 13.3 times earnings:

$$P/E = \frac{\$6.00}{\$0.45} = 13.3$$

The financial projections of the strategic plan put earnings for the current year (1984) at $0.82 per share and forecast that earnings would rise steadily over the period of the plan to $4.07 per share by 1989. If the earnings multiple (P/E) were to have stayed constant at 13.3, the stock could have been expected to rise to over $54.00 per share (13.3 x $4.07) by the end of the planning period!

Clearly, this appreciation is predicated on the company achieving its financial projections *and* the P/E retaining its value of 13.3 five years later. To that degree, it is conjectural and best not revealed to the investing public.

THE USE OF LEVERAGE

Leverage refers to the principle of borrowing to increase a company's capitalization. Capitalization consists of debt plus equity. The higher debt is relative to equity, the higher the leverage is said to be.

A measure of leverage is the *debt-to-equity ratio (D/E)*, which is given by:

$$D/E = \frac{\text{Debt}}{\text{Equity}}$$

Figure 9-2 is a plot of NBI's debt-to-equity ratio.

Prior to 1983, the company had negligible debt; hence the nominal values of D/E. In 1983, the company assumed $44 million of debt and its D/E jumped to the indicated value of 0.52. That infusion of capital was foreseen to be sufficient to sustain the business for three years (through 1985) and D/E was projected to decline over this period of time because the denominator of the ratio (equity) was projected to increase as retained earnings were being accumulated. Another $40 million of debt was forecast to be required in 1986, which bumped D/E to 0.76, its highest value over the time span of the strategic plan.

The debt-to-equity plot of Figure 9-2 is not difficult to grasp, but what does it really mean? How much debt is enough, or too much? What is an acceptable range of values for D/E? How much leverage is prudent?

Figure 9-2
Debt-to-Equity Ratio

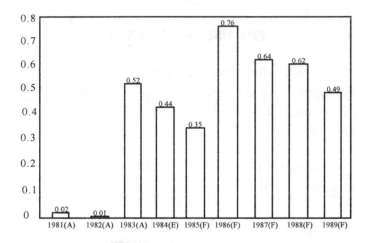

To answer these questions, one must realize that debt is merely a vehicle for increasing the investment base of a business beyond that contributed by the shareholders and retained earnings. Debt supplements equity to comprise the total investment with which the company has to work, the investment upon which ROI is calculated. The following expression captures this point:

$$Investment = Debt + Equity$$

Assume the following notations:

$$I = Investment$$
$$D = Debt$$
$$E = Equity$$

Then the foregoing expression can be written in algebraic notation as:

$$I = D + E$$

224

Plan For Profitability!

My view is that it is prudent to add debt (and thereby increase investment) *as long as there is incremental return on the investment*. Return on investment (ROI) is a function of net income, which takes into account both the operating profit generated by putting additional debt capital to work and the interest expense of borrowing the capital.

To reiterate, increased investment by adding debt is warranted as long as the increased investment yields an increase in return on investment (ROI). This concept is illustrated graphically by the plot of Figure 9-3. It is reasonable to increase investment as long as the slope of ROI versus I is positive (i.e., upward). The point where the slope falls to zero (levels off) is the point of diminishing return on investment. After this point, the slope turns negative (declines). Further investment is unwarranted, since it reduces ROI.

Figure 9-3
Incremental Return on Investment

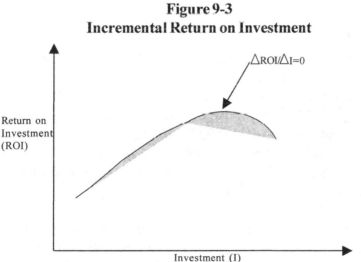

We can express this point of diminishing return mathematically. That point where the next increment of investment (Δ I) does not yield any incremental return on investment (Δ ROI)

is given by:

$$\frac{\Delta \text{ ROI}}{\Delta \text{ I}} = 0$$

To wrap up the concept of leverage, bear with me while I perform one more mathematical manipulation:

$$\text{ROE} = \frac{\text{Net Income}}{\text{Equity}} = \frac{\text{NI}}{\text{E}}$$

$$\text{ROE} = \frac{\text{NI}}{\text{E}} \times \frac{(\text{D}+\text{E})}{(\text{D}+\text{E})}$$

$$\text{ROE} = \frac{(\text{D}+\text{E})}{\text{E}} \times \frac{\text{NI}}{(\text{D}+\text{E})}$$

$$\text{ROE} = \frac{(\text{E}+\text{D})}{\text{E}} \times \frac{\text{NI}}{\text{I}}$$

$$\text{ROE} = (1 + \text{D/E}) \times \text{ROI}$$

In other words, return on equity (ROE) and return on investment (ROI) are interrelated by the degree to which the business is leveraged, the debt-to-equity ratio (D/E). If there is no debt (D/E = 0), both measures of return are obviously identical. As debt is added (D/E > 0), ROE is increased from its zero-debt value by a compound effect that consists of (1) the multiplier (1 + D/E) and (2) the increase in ROI that results from the increased debt.

At the point of diminishing return that we just discussed, although the multiplier (1 + D/E) is increasing, ROI is falling. It is possible to increase ROE beyond this point, but the compound effect of two increasing multipliers will have degenerated into the increasing leverage multiplier fighting against a decreasing ROI multiplier, with far less spectacular results.

Plan For Profitability!

To sum up the concept of leverage, the prudent use of debt can markedly increase the return on shareholders' equity. A good rule of thumb is to avoid adding debt if the increase in debt does not produce a demonstrable increase in return on total investment.

DEBT VERSUS EQUITY

In the preceding chapter, we explored the financial projections of Industrial Terminal Systems (ITS). You will recall that ITS was searching for an infusion of venture capital in the amount of $2 million. Wisely, the company elected not to address in its financial projections the issue of how much equity it would have to surrender to the venture capitalist in return for the funding, preferring to leave this issue to face-to-face negotiations.

The result of this tactical decision on the part of ITS was that the company's projected balance sheet displayed a cash shortfall of almost $500,000 in the first year of the forecast. (See Figure 8-5.) While this tactic may have been appropriate in the unique circumstances of ITS, its is rarely appropriate for most companies to project negative cash balances in their financial forecasts. Either debt or equity must be planned for to generate the cash. The question is: which one?

The answer to this question should be addressed in two steps:

1) Which funding vehicle should be assumed in the strategic plan?

2) Should the question of debt or equity be readdressed at that point in the future when the need for the capital is approaching?

With regard to this first question, it is easier to estimate the cost of borrowing at some time in the future than it is to estimate the cost of equity financing. Most companies can predict a rate of interest on their future long-term borrowing. Typically, this rate will be the prime rate at the time of borrowing plus an historical fixed *premium* over the prime rate that reflects the creditworthiness of the company.

So, the challenge is to project the prime rate over the planning horizon. This also is fairly straightforward, since the prime rate typically tracks a few points above the rate of inflation, the projection of which is one of the basic assumptions of the strategic plan. In short, when the planner assumes of the rate of inflation over the planning horizon, he also can (and should) forecast the prime rate and the company's projected borrowing rate.

By contrast, as we learned in the last chapter, equity financing requires that we address how many shares of stock the company will have to issue at some time in the future to generate the cash its needs at that time. This demands that we predict the market price of a share of the company's stock, which is given by:

$$\text{Share Price} = (\text{P/E}) \times \text{EPS}$$

Although there exists a forecast for EPS, the challenge is to project the price-to-earnings multiple of the company's stock at the time the capital is needed. P/E is, unfortunately, a function of not only the company's track record and prospects, but also of the strength or weakness of the overall securities market. I prefer to pass on predicting the performance of the stock market. For this reason, my preference is to always assume debt financing to generate capital if it is needed over the planning horizon.

To the second question posed above, as the time at which financing is needed approaches, the tradeoff of debt versus equity should definitely be addressed. There is far less uncertainty in the parameters of both approaches, since the deal is imminent. At a macro level, there are two considerations in the tradeoff, flexibility and EPS.

Debt is usually the more flexible alternative, in that debt can be retired with more impunity than equity. Retirements of debentures are far more prevalent than stock repurchases. So, if the need for additional capital is transient, debt will probably be the preferred alternative. On the other hand, if the additional capital will be retained as part of the company's long-term capital structure, equity may be appropriate.

The ultimate test in the tradeoff is that of resulting earnings per share (EPS). Remember that EPS is simply:

$$EPS = \frac{Net\ Income}{Shares\ Outstanding} = \frac{NI}{S}$$

If additional shares, ΔS, are issued in exchange for the capital, EPS will be reduced because the denominator of the above expression will increase as follows:

$$EPS = \frac{NI}{S + \Delta S}$$

The debt alternative will result in reduced EPS because the numerator of the expression will decrease by the after-tax cost of the additional interest on the debt. Say that $\triangle I$ is the additional interest that results from the new debt and that k is the marginal tax rate. Net income will be reduced as follows:

$$EPS = \frac{NI - (1-k)\,\triangle I}{S}$$

All things being equal, whichever approach dilutes earnings per share the least should be viewed as the preferred alternative.

OPERATING EFFICIENCY MEASUREMENTS

Return measurements such as ROS, ROI, ROE and EPS focus on the bottom line, net income, and its magnitude relative to revenues, investment, shareholders' equity and shares outstanding, respectively. The bottom line is, of course, the ultimate test of any profit-oriented business. Net income is, however, a superficial measurement in that it reveals little insight into how well or poorly the business is being run.

To be sure, if bottom line results are good, then the business is usually well run. If results are poor, however, we need some insight into why. Measurements of *operating efficiency* help to provide that insight.

Several measurements of efficiency were discussed in Chapter VII. Among them, *revenues per employee* is a general indicator of employee efficiency. Its trend over the long term should be gradually upward, because the principle of the learning curve tells us that companies should become more efficient with experience. Inflation also supports an upward trend. Employee wages increase over time, and so also then must revenues to pay the increased wages and still turn a profit.

Plan For Profitability!

A clear danger signal is a declining trend in revenues per employee. This may mean that prices need to be increased, especially if the decline in revenues per employee is also accompanied by declining gross margins. More often than not, however, declining revenues per employee signal that a company's headcount is simply too large to sustain the projected volume of business. This is usually a paramount early warning signal that headcount needs to be reduced, either by a hiring freeze and natural attrition, or by layoff.

Discussed also in Chapter VII, *facility space per employee* is a coarse measure of how efficiently the company's facilities are being utilized. An upward trend generally warns that the company has excess space and should look into disposing of a portion of its facilities.

Gross margin was explored in detail at the outset of this chapter. A downward trend is clearly a danger signal, perhaps the clearest and loudest of all such signals. The gross margin of a company is meaningful only when it is compared with the margins of the company's direct competitors. A significant competitive disadvantage in gross margin must be viewed as a major weakness.

The efficiency of asset and liability management can be tracked by *inventory turns*, *days receivables* and *days payables*, all of which were covered in Chapter VIII. Inventory turns should be kept high to tie up as little working capital as possible in inventory. A decreasing trend in inventory turns should be eyed with concern. Days receivables should be kept low and an increasing trend is unfavorable. Days payable should be kept high and a downtrend is undesirable.

As we just discussed, *discretionary expenses* are those functional expenses below the gross margin line and include

Marketing, Engineering, and General and Administrative (G&A) expenses. The discretion applies to how much expense should be applied to each function, not to the functions themselves, which are essential in most enterprises. How much should be expended in each category is dependent on the size of the business. A meaningful measurement of discretionary expenses is the expense relative to revenues (expressed as a percentage), as follows:

$$\text{Marketing (\%)} = \frac{\text{Marketing Expenses}}{\text{Revenues}}$$

$$\text{Engineering (\%)} = \frac{\text{Engineering Expenses}}{\text{Revenues}}$$

$$\text{G\&A (\%)} = \frac{\text{G\&A Expenses}}{\text{Revenues}}$$

Let us return to NBI and use operating efficiency measurements to try to gain some insight into the two questions that we posed earlier in this chapter. Recall that the two questions were:

1) What caused the precipitous drop in ROS from 11% in 1982 to 3.7% in 1983?

2) Is it reasonable to forecast a jump of 1.8 points in ROS in 1988? If so, why?

Figure 9-4 is a tabulation of selected efficiency measurements for the company.

Figure 9-4
Selected Operating Efficiency Measurements

	1981(A)	1982(A)	1983(A)	1984(E)	1985(F)	1986(F)	1987(F)	1988(F)	1989(F)
Gross Margin	58.2%	58.1%	54.7%	55.0%	55.5%	55.6%	55.4%	56.9%	58.0%
Inventory Turns	2.2	2.0	1.6	1.7	1.8	1.9	2.0	2.0	2.0
Days Receivables	108	117	116	114	98	99	104	96	110
Days Payables	106	76	86	90	89	90	92	93	92
Marketing	5.2%	6.3%	9.2%	8.1%	7.5%	8.9%	7.7%	7.6%	7.7%
Engineering	24.1%	24.4%	29.3%	27.2%	28.2%	28.9%	29.5%	28.4%	29.3%
G&A	10.1%	10.2%	12.2%	10.8%	10.2%	10.0%	9.7%	9.3%	8.9%

To address the first question about the drop of 7.3 points in ROS from 1982 to 1983, look at the columns of Figure 9-4 for those two years. Four elements combined in 1983 to add 13.2 points of expense relative to 1982 figures. These four elements are summarized in Figure 9-5.

Figure 9-5
1982-83 Expense Deterioration

	1982(A)	1983(A)	Deterioration
Gross Margin (%)	58.1	54.7	3.4
Marketing (%)	24.4	29.3	4.9
Engineering (%)	6.3	9.2	2.9
G&A (%)	10.2	12.2	2.0
Total			**13.2**

In the company's 1983 annual report, the bulk of these increases in cost were attributed to the introduction of a new product line. With that kind of deterioration in the operating statement, the company was fortunate to have held the decline in its ROS to 7.3 points.

Scanning your eyes across the gross margin row of Figure 9-4, note that for the five-year stretch from 1983 through 1987, gross margin was projected to be fairly flat just above the 55% level. In 1988 and 1989, however, it was inexplicably forecast to jump 1.5 and 1.1 points, respectively. This hope of improved margins at the end of the planning horizon was the major factor behind the optimistic ROS expectations in the last two years of the forecast.

Subsequent investigation into a rationale to support the increased margin revealed that there was no program in place to improve margins over the period of the plan. In other words, the projected increases in margins were based on little more than hope. Remember Hargrave's Law. Positive action is required to improve margins. They do not improve on their own initiative.

TREND ANALYSIS

In addition to assessing the magnitude of key indicators, one can also gain insight into the validity of a long-range forecast by examining the trends of the key parameters. In so doing, it is helpful to view a few years of historical data to detect past and current trends. Recall that Hargrave's Law states that unfavorable trends perpetuate themselves in the absence of decisive corrective actions, while favorable trends require continual reinforcement. Even if you are skeptical of my Law, you must surely agree that it leads to diligent business management.

The most famous of all adverse trends is the *hockey stick*, the classical form of which is depicted in Figure 9-6. Hockey sticks come in all sizes and shapes, and can apply to any relevant parameter. In the example shown, the parameter is net income.

Plan For Profitability!

Figure 9-6
Alarm Patterns in Forecasts:
The Classical Hockey Stick

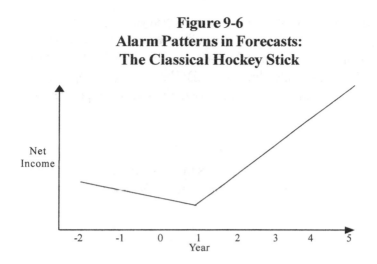

The story that accompanies the hockey stick invariably has a plot comparable to the following: An SBU has a history of steadily declining profitability. Consistent with that trend, net income in the year in which the strategic plan is being prepared (Year 0) is budgeted to be less than the year before. If this trend is to be reversed (provided it can be), decisive steps need to be taken without delay. However, the General Manager of the SBU submits a strategic plan that shows one more year of net income decline (Year 1) and *then* a turn-around. The shape of the resulting graph resembles a hockey stick.

Hockey sticks should be viewed with skepticism. There may be valid reasons for such forecasts, but my view is that they should be judged guilty until proven innocent. Two years is a long time to turn a business around in today's aggressive business climate. The chances are that, if it takes two years, it will not be turned around.

An even more insidious form of the hockey stick is the creeping hockey stick, suggested in Figure 9-7. The creeping hockey stick crept up on me several years ago when one of the SBU's in my company submitted a strategic plan and accompanying revenue forecast (in Year -2) in the shape suggested by the dotted line. The SBU had negligible operating history, so that there was no prior data to help me spot trends.

Figure 9-7
Alarm Patterns in Forecasts:
The Creeping Hockey Stick

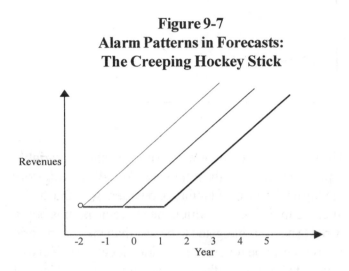

The following year (Year -1), the SBU turned in a forecast that deferred its revenue growth by one year and essentially slid the prior year's revenue projections one year to the right, as shown by the light solid line. In the third year (Year 0), the General Manager submitted a forecast that again delayed revenue growth, translated the growth curve another year to the right, and produced the obvious hockey stick described by the heavy solid line. Perhaps I should have spotted the hockey stick earlier than the third year, but I can assure you that the General Manager's third strategic plan was rejected and that he was directed to take corrective actions.

In 1979, I reviewed the strategic plan of Fairchild Industries, a Fortune 500 aerospace company with annual revenues of around $600 million. Fairchild had an interesting approach to planning. They specified an annual rate of growth that they expected the company as a whole to achieve over the planning horizon. Then, they directed the General Managers of the SBU's to submit their individual plans, but without any guidelines that translated the company's overall growth objective into objectives for each of the SBU's.

Inevitably, the sums of the plans of the SBU's fell short of the company's growth objectives, creating a *gap* that was identified in the financial projections as "undefined products." This is suggested by Figure 9-8. Needless to say, history proved that the company tracked the consolidated SBU projections more closely than the corporate objective, for there were no identified strategies and programs in the plan to make those future undefined products a reality. The company had convoluted the logical flow of preparing a strategic plan by starting with financial projections rather than letting them be the product of thoughtful analysis.

Figure 9-8
Alarm Patterns in Forecasts: The Gap

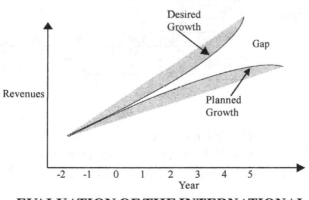

EVALUATION OF THE INTERNATIONAL

MICROWIDGETS PLAN

The plan is finished, or is it? Of the many talented people who have worked for me over the years, I found that it was at this point in the strategic planning process that many of them exhibited a curious lack of closure. They worked diligently and intelligently up to this point, the completion of the financials. Then they proudly presented the final product to their clients without, oddly, taking the time to study the results to see what conclusions could be drawn from them.

An experienced CEO, Bill Portes always makes it a practice at this point in the agenda of trying to view the plan through the eyes of his clients, the Board of Directors of International Microwidgets. Figure 9-9 is one of the tools he uses for his analysis, a tabulation of the return measurements discussed earlier in this chapter, viz., Gross Margin, ROS, ROE, ROI, EPS and the debt-to-equity ratio (D/E).

Figure 9-9
International Microwidgets Return Measurements

Year	-2(A)	-1(A)	0(E)	1(F)	2(F)	3(F)
Gross Margin	60%	59%	58%	57%	59%	61%
ROS	6.9%	5.9%	5.0%	3.3%	4.8%	6.3%
ROE	6.7%	6.2%	5.8%	3.9%	6.5%	9.2%
ROI	6.7%	6.2%	5.8%	3.1%	5.3%	7.6%
EPS	$2.31	$2.30	$2.29	$1.65	$2.81	$4.25
D/E	0	0	0	0.26	0.23	0.21

The first observation that he makes is that, with the exception of D/E, each of the measurements exhibits the characteristics of a hockey stick. There is a decline in the return parameter in Years -2 through 1, and then a sharp rebound in

Plan For Profitability!

Years 2 and 3. Figure 9-10 illustrates the point by displaying the hockey stick for one of the parameters, Gross Margin.

Figure 9-10
International Microwidgets Gross Margin

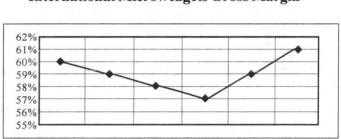

Portes knows that the Directors of International Microwidgets will view the projections for the coming year (Year 1) with concern, particularly the drop in EPS from the plateau of $2.30 to $1.65. Portes believes that his analysis of the situation is sound. Gross margin has been in steady decline for three years, dropping about a point per year. As a result, ROS, ROE and ROI have all fallen. Only increased revenues have prevented a drop in earnings, which have been flat over the period. Decisive actions need to be taken to reverse the trend of declining margin.

Since you have been following the development of the plan, you know that the actions to improve margins consist of setting up (1) a plant to manufacture semiconductors internally and (2) plants to assemble microwidgets in China and Eastern Europe. However, the improvements in margin will not be realized overnight. It will take a year for the plants to come on line; hence, the company must suffer through one more year of decline in gross margin before the efficiencies of the new plants can be realized. On top of that, interest on the debt for the new plants will clobber earnings in the intervening year, depressing net income and EPS by over 25%.

On the positive side, the payoff to these actions promises to be dramatic. In just three years, gross margin, ROE, ROI and EPS should all be at levels greater than those of two years ago. Earnings should be $4.25 per share, almost double the current level. Return on shareholders' equity should reach 9.2%, reflecting leveraging the shareholders' investment with debt. Faced with the alternative of doing nothing and watching margins continue to decline, Bill Portes believes that his course of action is sound and that the Board will concur with his proposed strategy.

He continues to scrutinize the financials by examining the historical and projected operating efficiency of the company. Recall that the relevant parameters are revenue per employee, facility space per employee, inventory turns, days receivables, days payables, and Marketing, Engineering and G&A as a percent of revenue. This tabulation is shown in Figure 9-11.

Figure 9-11
International Microwidgets
Operating Efficiency Measurements

Year	-2(A)	-1(A)	0(E)	1(F)	2(F)	3(F)
Revenue/ Employee (thousands)	$200	$213	$222	$232	$231	$247
Space/ Employee (sq. ft.)	250	250	250	292	250	250
Inventory Turns	1.2	1.2	1.3	1.3	1.2	1.2
Days Receivables	61	61	61	61	61	61
Days Payables	184	177	172	169	177	188
Marketing/ Revenues	25%	25%	25%	25%	25%	25%
Engineering/ Revenues	12%	12%	12%	12%	12%	12%
G&A/Revenues	8%	8%	8%	8%	8%	8%

Plan For Profitability!

As Bill Portes reviews his company's historical and projected operating efficiency, he makes a few notes. Revenue per employee increases steadily over the period of the plan, save for a transient downturn in Year 2 when the employees for the new plants are on board but not yet up to full productivity. Facility space per employee is level at 250 square feet, except for a spike to 292 square feet at the end of Year 1 when the new plants have been completed but not yet fully staffed by employees.

Inventory turns have stagnated at 1.2-1.3 times per year with no improvement in sight. Portes views this as unacceptable in light of the progress that many companies have made in implementing just-in-time (JIT) inventory control to reduce the raw materials component of inventory. He is, however, reluctant to address this issue at a time when the company's manufacturing operations are slated to undergo dramatic change and makes a note to make improving inventory turns a priority issue once the semiconductor and assembly plants have settled into operation.

Receivables of 61 days duration, about two months, are lower than the industry average. Although Portes would prefer to see some gradual reduction in this figure over the horizon of the plan, he considers this an issue of secondary priority. The figure that really concerns him is days payable. Historically, International Microwidgets has been able to defer payments to its vendors by an average of six months, chiefly because of the volume of its purchases. This company will surely not be able to enjoy such a float of its payables when it manufactures rather than purchases its semiconductors. Again, however, Portes decides to defer this issue until the manufacturing plans for the new plants are complete.

At 25%, 12% and 8% of revenues, respectively, Marketing, Engineering and General and Administrative expenses are unremarkable and consistent with expense ratios of the company's competitors. Bill Portes decides that he has a strategic plan that can be presented to the Board of Directors. The only remaining task is to formulate the proposal for the acquisition of General Microwidgets. We will rejoin International Microwidgets and that topic in the chapter after next.

SUMMARY

In evaluating your strategic plan, keep the following points in mind:

- Among a group of competitors, the company with the highest gross margin is likely to be the most profitable and the market share leader.

- Net income is the single parameter most scrutinized by analysts. It forms the basis for return measurements such as ROS, ROI, ROE and EPS.

- Prudent use of debt permits a company to increase the return on shareholders' equity.

- If the financial projections indicate that cash is required over the planning horizon, debt should be assumed as the financing vehicle. The tradeoff of debt versus equity can always be made when the financing is imminent.

- Measurements of operating efficiency provide insight into how well the company is using its per sonnel, plant, working capital and discretionary resources.

- Unfavorable trends tend to continue unless positive action is taken to counter the trend. Favorable trends usually require reinforcement to be sustained.

- Hockey stick forecasts should be considered suspect until proven otherwise.

CHAPTER X
BEYOND STRATEGIC PLANNING

Good order is the foundation of all things.

Edmund Burke, 1790

Don't agonize. Organize.

Florynce R. Kennedy, 1973

Early to bed, early to rise, work like hell and organize.

Albert Gore, Jr. 1988

"Begin at the beginning," the King said, gravely, "and go till you come to the end; then stop." Perhaps, in Lewis Carroll's Wonderland, strategic planners, upon completing their plans, can stop and rest on their laurels until the planning cycle begins anew in the ensuing fiscal year. Not so in the real world.

In my experience, there is no slack period for planners. Upon completing the strategic plan, the planning focus usually shifts to the operational plan, which concentrates on the first year of the strategic plan and amplifies its activities into budgets and milestones for the ensuing year. I could write a separate book on operational planning and perhaps someday I will. For the time being, we will briefly cover operational planning in this chapter.

Another rewarding project is to assist the CEO in examining the organizational structure of the company to ascertain if it is optimized to implement the strategies and carry out the programs of the strategic plan. There is an antecedent relationship between the strategy of a company and the organization that the company establishes to carry out the strategy, as well as between the organizational structure and the skill and responsibility profiles of the individuals who staff the positions in the structure. I call this logical relationship *The Three S's* and we will also explore this concept in this chapter.

Frequently, programs are identified in the strategic plan that do not conveniently fall under the purview of any single SBU or organizational unit of the company. Among the activities in this category are acquisitions, divestitures, startups and shutdowns. Collectively, these projects are usually referred to as *Business Development* or *Corporate Development* activities, and I shall use the latter term.

The high profile of these projects necessitates that they be spearheaded by a representative of the CEO who has a global view of the company, its strategies and its objectives. As a result, the planner's role is often expanded to assume the leadership of these key Corporate Development projects. Moreover, the priority of Corporate Development projects is such that they cannot be pursued at leisure in slack periods between plans but must be must be pursued with urgency, often in parallel with strategic and operational planning. My experience as Vice President for Corporate Planning and Development was that fully two-thirds of my time was spent on Corporate Development projects. A requisite of the position is to be able to keep several balls in the air at the same time.

THE OPERATIONAL PLAN

We discussed the annual planning cycle in the early part of Chapter II. Recall that the preparation of the strategic plan precedes that of the operational plan. The operational plan focuses on the year ahead, the first year of the strategic plan. Figure 10-1, reproduced from Chapter II, illustrates the chronological relationship between the two plans.

Figure 10-1
The Annual Corporate Planning Cycle

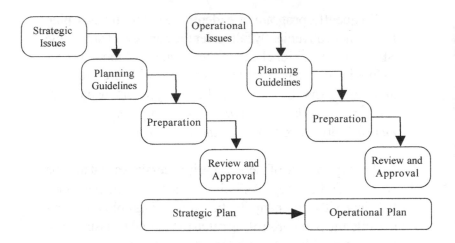

Strategic planning is *macro* planning. The plan is developed from the *top down*, beginning with the concept of the mission of the company and a holistic examination of the market.

In contrast, operational planning is *micro* planning. The plan is developed from the *bottom up* by those managers whose performance will subsequently be measured against the plan in the coming year. The essential elements of measurement within the operational plan include (1) a translation of the company's goals for the year into specific goals for each component of the organization and (2) detailed revenue and expense budgets for each cost center.

As an example of an operational plan, I have chosen CASI-RUSCO, a company that I led for five years. My assignment began in early 1986 when I took over as President of Rusco Electronic Systems, a California-based manufacturer of com

246

puter-based access control systems. Access control systems monitor and grant (or deny) personnel access to facilities. Any time that you insert a card in a reader to gain access to a building, you interact with an access control system.

Formerly the market leader in access control, Rusco had fallen on hard times due to a bloated expense structure, an obsolescent product line and declining sales. In the year preceding my arrival, the company had lost $5.8 million on revenues of only $19 million. Clearly, my first task was to turn the company around, which I did within 18 months, notwithstanding the fact that annual revenues continued to sag to $17.5 million in the year in which I arrived.

The next step was to inject some new technology into the company without delay to position the company to compete again in its market and reverse the decline in sales. I concluded that the only realistic way to accomplish this was by acquisition, since Rusco had neither the time nor the resources to catch up technologically on its own. I identified a small company in Florida called Computer Application Systems Inc. (CASI) that had the requisite leading-edge technology, acquired the company in 1987 and renamed the combined company CASI-RUSCO.

The ensuing three years were spent in moving all of the combined company's operations out of California and consolidating them in Florida, restructuring and expanding the channels of distribution, and developing a next-generation access control system that was designed to leapfrog the competition. These bold measures paid off. By the mid-1990's, CASI-RUSCO had grown to become the leading access control company in the world.

Figure 10-2 is an excerpt from CASI-RUSCO's operational plan for the year 1990. This plan was formulated in the fourth quarter of 1989. This figure displays the top level of the company's revenue and expense budget for the year 1990. Four years of history are displayed for comparative purposes, three years (1986-88) of actual results and one year (1989) of estimated results.

A useful technique in budgeting is to express every item of expense in each year as a percentage of the revenues for that year. Then, the aim in the year being budgeted is to reduce each expense item to the lowest value *as a percentage of revenues* in the time frame of the historical retrospective. The bold-faced expense items in the exhibit denote the lowest value over the time frame for each item of expense. Thus, in the example of Figure 10-2, Cost of Goods Sold reached its nadir of 46% (of revenues) in 1987 and the budget for 1990 almost reaches this objective at 47%. Marketing, Engineering and G&A are, however, budgeted at their lowest percentage of revenues over the five-year time span.

Figure 10-2
A Top-Level Budget
($ in thousands)

	1986(A)		1987(A)		1988(A)		1989(E)		1990(F)	
Revenues	17,535	100%	20,340	100%	24,874	100%	23,096	100%	25,700	100%
Cost of Goods Sold	9,152	52%	9,387	**46%**	12,513	50%	13,459	58%	12,201	47%
Gross Profit	8,383	48%	10,953	54%	12,361	50%	9,637	42%	13,499	53%
Marketing	5,639	32%	4,969	24%	5,946	24%	4,722	20%	4,750	**18%**
Engineering	3,189	18%	2,379	12%	2,519	10%	2,933	12%	2,672	**10%**
General & Administrative	2,522	14%	2,308	11%	2,206	9%	1,780	8%	1,845	**7%**
Total Expenses	11,350	65%	9,656	47%	10,668	43%	9,335	40%	9,267	36%
Operating Profit	(2,967)	-17%	1,297	6%	1,693	7%	302	1%	4,232	16%
Interest and Other Expenses	458	**3%**	1,213	6%	3,906	16%	2,880	12%	3,627	14%
Pre-Tax Profit	(3,425)	-20%	84	0%	(2,213)	-9%	(2,578)	-11%	605	2%
Income Taxes	-	0%	-	0%	-	0%	-	0%	-	0%
Net Income	(3,425)	-20%	84	0%	(2,213)	-9%	(2,578)	-11%	605	2%
Average Headcount	265		256		202		168		159	
Revenues/Employee	66		79		123		137		**162**	

Plan For Profitability!

The brief history that I shared with you about the turn-around of Rusco and the acquisition of CASI is reflected in the five-year time span of Figure 10-2. Note the following aspects of this historical picture:

- CASI was acquired in late 1987. Only a portion of its sales were reflected in the revenue figure for 1987, but all of its contribution to sales revenues were counted in the 1988 figure. Hence, the increase in sales attributable to CASI was, at the very least, the difference between 1988 and 1986 sales, about $7.3 million. In actuality, it was greater, since sales of Rusco products continued their decline over this period.

- To acquire CASI, Rusco had to take on debt to pay for the company and, with it, interest expense. Moreover, there were significant relocation expenses over the 1988-90 time period as the company moved all of its operations from California to Florida. The result was a steep jump in Interest and Other Expenses from 3% of revenues in 1986 to 12-16% in 1988-90. With the debt load that the company carried, there was no way that it could reduce this line item of expense to the low level of 1986.

- One of the keys to turning Rusco around was reducing expenses. In most companies, the single greatest element of expense is people. Note that, over the five-year time span, the company was able to increase its revenues by almost 50% while decreasing its headcount by 40%. As a result, revenues increased from $66,000 to $162,000 per employee over this period.

249

Figure 10-3 shows the breakout of a detailed budget, in this case, for the Marketing organization. This budget was prepared by the Vice President of Marketing, who prepared it with the concurrent commitment to operate within it for the ensuing year. Note that the aim of minimizing expenses relative to revenues is achieved for most of the line items of expense (the bold-faced entries). Note also that personnel costs (salaries, commissions and payroll fringes) comprise almost two-thirds of the entire budget for the department, reinforcing the observation about the significant cost of people.

Figure 10-3
A Detailed Budget
($ in thousands)

	1986(A)		1987(A)		1988(A)		1989(E)		1990(F)	
Salaries and Commissions	2,855	16.30%	2,420	11.90%	2,525	10.15%	2,336	10.11%	2,382	**9.27%**
Payroll Fringes	691	3.95%	599	2.94%	740	2.97%	580	2.51%	621	**2.42%**
Travel and Entertainment	529	3.02%	589	2.90%	743	2.99%	497	**2.15%**	555	2.16%
Depreciation	64	**0.37%**	85	0.42%	242	0.97%	171	0.74%	114	0.44%
Rents	195	1.11%	177	0.87%	207	0.90%	131	0.57%	106	**0.41%**
Telecommunications	313	1.79%	220	1.08%	229	0.92%	207	0.90%	222	**0.86%**
Advertising and Promotion	398	2.27%	376	1.85%	699	2.81%	394	1.71%	301	**1.17%**
Outside Services	83	0.47%	120	0.59%	141	0.57%	74	0.32%	42	**0.16%**
Freight and Postage	101	0.58%	80	0.39%	115	0.46%	39	0.17%	32	**0.12%**
Data Processing	153	0.87%	172	0.85%	83	**0.33%**	129	0.56%	234	0.91%
Recruiting and Relocation	10	**0.06%**	20	0.10%	53	0.21%	86	0.37%	85	0.33%
Materials and Supplies	56	0.32%	51	0.25%	52	0.21%	47	0.20%	33	**0.13%**
Other Expenses	191	1.09%	60	0.29%	114	0.46%	31	0.13%	23	**0.09%**
Total Marketing Expenses	5,639	32.20%	4,969	24.43%	5,943	23.89%	4,722	21.45%	4,750	18.48%

THE THREE S's

Once the strategic plan has been prepared, the insightful CEO reassesses the structure of his organization to assure himself that the structure of the organization is still appropriate to accomplish the programs and goals outlined in the strategic plan. Alfred Chandler first articulated the concept that strategy determines organizational structure. He wrote:

Plan For Profitability!

"The thesis that different organizational forms result from different types of growth can be stated more precisely if the planning and carrying out of such growth is considered a *strategy*, and the organization designed to administer these enlarged activities and resources, a *structure*. *Strategy* can be defined as the determination of the basic long-term goals and objectives of an enterprise, and the adoption of courses of action and the allocation of resources for carrying out these goals. . . .

"*Structure* can be defined as the design of an organization through which the enterprise is administered. . . . The thesis produced from these several propositions is that structure follows strategy."[1]

If structure follows strategy, then *staffing* follows structure, where staffing is defined as the selection and training of the personnel to staff the organizational structure. It seems reasonable to me that the requirements for human resources in the form of job descriptions and headcount requirements are ultimately determined by the organizational structure devised to administer the programs of the strategic plan.

In sum, strategy determines structure. Structure determines staffing. The logical flow of these *three S's* is shown in Figure 10-4.

Figure 10-4
The Three S's

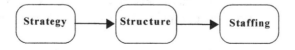

[1] Alfred D. Chandler, Jr., Strategy and Structure: Chapters in the History of the American Industrial Enterprise, Massachusetts Institute of Technology, 1962

The thesis of the three S's is so obvious that it borders on the simplistic. It is amazing to me, however, how many otherwise thoughtful executives transpose these cause-and-effect relationships by setting up organizational structures prior to having developed strategic plans or by contorting organizational structures to fit the talents of existing personnel. I have observed numerous organizations that were designed to accommodate the strengths (and weaknesses) of certain executives rather than to fulfill the company's strategies and programs, with resulting inefficiencies.

The task of examining the current organization, assessing its ability to carry out the strategic plan and making recommendations for change is frequently assumed by the planner. While there are good books on organizational development, you may be interested in my view of the subject. To begin, it is beneficial to understand the basic types of organizational structures and the difference between line and staff functions.

ORGANIZATIONAL STRUCTURES

One extreme of organizational structure is the *functional organization*. In such an organization, the company is partitioned into the major functions, disciplines or duties that the company must perform to conduct its business. Figure 10-5 is a diagram of a representative functional organization with six major functions:

- Engineering, which designs and develops the products that comprise the business of the company.

- Manufacturing, which converts the engineering designs into manufacturable products and produces them in volumes and to schedules consistent with the demands of the customers.

- Marketing, which ascertains the requirements of customers, specifies the product requirements to Engineering, sets production requirements for Manufacturing, and sells and distributes the products to customers.

- Finance, which monitors, anticipates, and controls the incoming and outgoing flow of the company's funds, and maintains the associated financial records.

- Human Resources, which assures that the personnel requirements of the company are met and administers employee-related programs such as benefits, personnel records, training, hiring, and the like.

- Central Services, a broad function which provides all of the non-human resources that the company requires to operate, including manufacturing and office space and equipment, furnishings, office supplies, utilities, telecommunications, computers, etc.

Figure 10-5
A Typical Functional Organization

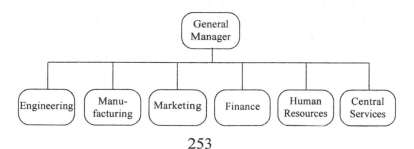

Functional organizations are prevalent among those companies that focus on a single product, a family of similar products or a single market. In other words, a company that organizes itself along functional lines is usually a self-contained Strategic Business Unit.

As a rule, the smaller the organization, the more likely it is to be functionally organized. Functional structures can, however, be found in very large organizations. For example, the billion-dollar aircraft engine business of General Electric in the 1970's was structured predominantly along functional lines. This was not surprising when one considers that this business produced a family of similar products (commercial and military aircraft engines) for a set of similar customers (domestic and foreign airframe manufacturers) in competition with primarily two competitors (Rolls Royce and Pratt and Whitney).

At the other extreme of the structural spectrum is the *business-* or *product-oriented organization,* illustrated in Figure 10-6. In this case, the primary subdivision of the company is into SBU's, i.e., discrete groupings of products or businesses, with some degree of homogeneity within each group, such as common markets, customers, product functions or technologies. Each group is essentially autonomous of the other groups and is functionally self-sufficient, with its own internal capabilities in the areas of engineering, manufacturing, marketing, finance, human resources and central services. In general, the larger the company, the more likely that it is organized along product or business lines. Large multi-business or conglomerate entities such as General Electric are excellent examples of this type of organization.

Plan For Profitability!

Figure 10-6
A Typical Product-Oriented Organization

Between the two foregoing extremes are the *hybrid* and *matrix organizations*, which are suggested by the diagrams of Figures 10-7 and 10-8. The hybrid organization, as its name implies, is partially a functional structure and partially a product structure. In the example of Figure 10-7, each product business organization has its own internal engineering, manufacturing and marketing resources, but relies upon corporate finance, human resources and central services for these functions.

The matrix organization is a special case of the hybrid structure, in that fairly complete functional and product organizations co-exist within the same company. As illustrated in Figure 10-8, each product group draws the resources it requires from each of the functional groups. The resulting row-and-column array in the figure is referred to in mathematics as a *matrix*, hence the name.

Figure 10-7
A Typical Hybrid Organization

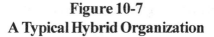
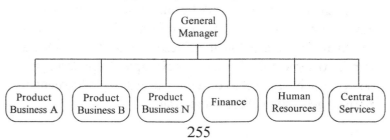

Figure 10-8
A Typical Matrix Organization

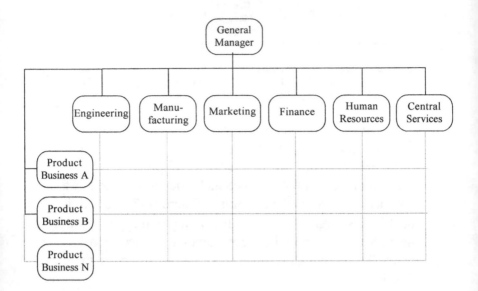

Companies in which the resource requirements of the product groups fluctuate widely and independently of one another frequently employ matrix organizations. The matrix structure permits the company to allocate its functional resources among the product groups such that the resources are deployed for the maximum benefit of the company as a whole.

General Electric's aircraft engine business, described earlier as a functional organization, had in reality some of the features of a matrix organization. There were strong product management groups within the business (viz., commercial engines, military engines, etc.) that, in effect, influenced the allocation of the available functional resources to the priorities at hand. At some point in time, for example, engineering resources might have been concentrated on the development of the next generation of commercial air craft engines, while concurrently the bulk of manufacturing resources were devoted to the production of military engines.

LINE AND STAFF FUNCTIONS

A concept that is infrequently emphasized in business curricula is the contrast between *line and staff functions*. In all probability, these terms have their roots in military organizations, where the fighting troops comprised the line and the staff provided military support to the commanders (and hence indirectly to the line). It is interesting to note that, although the line troops arguably could function without staff support, such support clearly enhances the line's fighting ability. On the other hand, if there were no line troops, there would be no need at all for staff support.

The military terminology has carried over into business with high parallel. Line functions are those which are directly involved in bringing a company's goods or services to market. Line components are necessary to the conduct of the business. Without them, vital links in the chain of the company's business are missing.

With reference to the six typical functions depicted in Figure 10-5, Engineering, Manufacturing and Marketing are line functions. Finance, Human Resources and Central Services are staff functions. The staff functions support the General Manager and the line operations. Without the goods or services that the line operations produce and provide to the market, the company could not conduct its business, and there would be no need for personnel (Human Resources), financial records (Finance), or facilities, equipment and supplies (Central Services). In sum, without the line functions, staff functions have no *raison d'etre* whatsoever.

Lee E. Hargrave, Jr.

A REPRESENTATIVE COMPANY
ORGANIZATION

Now to put all of this organizational theory together in the form of an actual company structure. Shown in Figure 10-9 is the upper tier of organization (circa 1983) of Storage Technology Corporation, a large manufacturer of computer systems and peripherals. At first glance the structure would appear to be functional in nature, and it is primarily so, except that a matrix interrelationship exists among the five elements across the bottom of the chart. Note that two of these functions have not been previously introduced:

Figure 10-9
Actual Company Organization

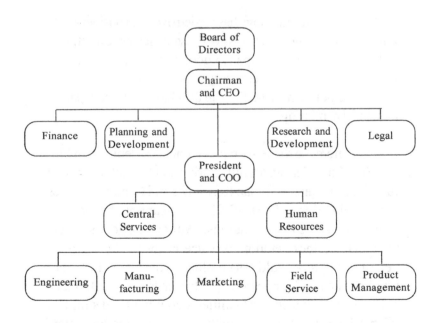

- Field Service, which encompassed the mainte-
nance and repair of the company's products at its
customers' installations. Because of the sheer size
of this effort in this company, Field Service was
broken out as a first-tier function, versus its in-
corporation within Marketing as would normally
be the case.

- Product Management, which was responsible for
anticipating and making the key decisions for each
of the company's products from inception through
end of life, including such issues as product speci-
fications, allocation of engineering resources, production volumes, product line profitability, and the
introduction and discontinuance of products. With
reference to the matrix organization of Figure 10-
8, Product Management may be viewed as the
rows of a matrix in which Engineering, Manufacturing, Marketing and Field Service are the columns.

Our representative organization contains three additional
components that have not been discussed to this point:

- Legal, which is self-explanatory in nature. Since
this company was large (of a size sufficient to be
included in the Fortune 500), it both needed and
could afford to maintain an internal legal staff.
Smaller companies generally do not have internal
attorneys and rely upon external counsel for their
legal needs.

- Research and Development, which embraced
basic and applied research and advanced development.

- Corporate Planning and Development, which encompassed strategic planning, operational planning and corporate development projects.

As a company increases in size, it becomes increasingly more difficult for a single individual to manage the day-to-day activities of the business and concurrently to determine, initiate and track those activities which are essential to the long-range positioning of the business. To return to the military parallel, it is difficult for most commanders to narrow their sights to the *tactics* of the battles at hand and simultaneously to develop and implement *strategies* that will ultimately win the war. In war or in business, the human tendency is to focus on immediate operations and to defer longer-range tasks, to their inevitable detriment.

The most common organizational remedy for this dilemma is to divide the position of General Manager into a *Chief Executive Officer (CEO)* and a *Chief Operating Officer (COO)*, with the latter normally reporting to the former. The COO concentrates on and is responsible for the short-term activities (operations) of the company, thereby freeing the CEO to focus on longer-range projects. In the example of Figure 10-9, the COO is given the title of President and the CEO is concurrently the Chairman of the Board of Directors.

The line of demarcation between what constitutes line and staff functions is not sharp. Staff functions often contain elements of line responsibilities and the converse is also true. In my opinion, the organization of Figure 10-9 consists of six line functions and seven staff functions, as follows:

- Line: CEO, COO, Engineering, Field Service, Manufacturing and Marketing

- Staff: Central Services, Corporate Planning and Development, Finance, Human Resources, Legal, Product Management, and Research and Development

Let me give an example of the subjective aspects of the foregoing classification. One could convincingly argue that Research and Development is a line function, the results of which are necessary inputs to the Engineering Department. However, companies generally prioritize their R&D projects according to maximum expected payoff and devote their resources to only a subset of their technological needs, electing to be followers in the other technological areas. In fact, some companies eschew R&D altogether and adopt conscious strategies of following the technological leaders in their industries. Hence, in my view, Research and Development is an elective (as opposed to a necessary) activity, and accordingly it belongs in the category of a staff function.

THE CONCEPT OF CORPORATE DEVELOPMENT

From Figure 10-9 and the accompanying text, we have established that Corporate Planning and Development is a staff function that usually reports (if it is properly positioned within the organization) directly to the Chief Executive Officer, i.e., to that executive who is responsible for the future of the enterprise. As we have discussed, the function consists of two activities, with the latter dependent upon the outcome of the former:

- Strategic Planning, which is the process of determining the most appropriate direction for the evolution of the company's business, and identifying

261

those steps that must be taken in the near term to initiate (or continue) the evolution. One of the first steps in strategic planning is to identify the SBU's that comprise the company. Operational planning usually also falls under the scope of Strategic Planning.

- Corporate Development, which is a generic term for those strategic projects that are company-wide in scope and impact. The most frequent examples of corporate development projects involve either pruning a business or product line from the company (e.g., by divestiture) or adding one by acquisition or by starting up an entirely new venture.

We will elaborate on Corporate Development in the next chapter.

SUMMARY

The following are the highlights of the chapter that you have just read:

- Strategic planners frequently find themselves involved in activities that are interrelated to strategic planning. Among these are operational planning, organizational development and corporate development.

- Operational planning is a bottom-up process, in contrast to strategic planning, which is top-down. The managers who must live with and perform to the resulting milestones and budgets prepare the plan. Cost-conscious budgeters strive to minimize each item of expense relative to revenues.

- A company's strategy should determine its organizational structure. In turn, its structure should determine the aptitudes of the personnel that fill the organization.

- Types of organizational structures include functional, product-oriented, hybrid and matrix. Functions within an organization are usually characterized as either line or staff functions.

- Corporate development encompasses those projects that are company-wide in scope and impact. Among them are acquisitions, divestitures, startups and shutdowns.

CHAPTER XI
CORPORATE DEVELOPMENT

Tis money that begets money.

English Proverb

Deals are my art form. Other people paint beautifully on canvas or write wonderful poetry. I like making deals, preferably big deals.

Donald Trump, 1987

Sometimes your best investments are the ones you don't make.

Donald Trump, 1987

Corporate Development (also called Business Development) encompasses those projects that are company-wide in scope and do not logically fall under the purview of one of the business or functional units of the company. Most of these projects involve entering new businesses or exiting existing ones. Corporate Development projects are often identified in the strategic planning process, but they sometimes come to the attention of the company in a fortuitous manner.

ENTERING AND EXITING BUSINESSES

Figure 11-1 presents an elemental view of the options that a company has when it decides to enter a new business or exit an existing one. The two columns of this four-block matrix represent entry and exit. The two rows represent the means by which the entry or exit is accomplished, either externally or internally.

Plan For Profitability!

Entering a business by external means (the upper left block of the matrix) entails either an *acquisition* or a *merger*. The difference between a merger and an acquisition is chiefly one of form, which we will explore shortly. Alternatively, a company may choose to enter a new business via internal means (the lower left block), which is commonly referred to as a *startup*. In between these two extremes is the *joint venture*, which combines internal resources with one or more external partners. Joint ventures are especially attractive when the technology or know-how to enter the business resides among two or more companies or when the price tag to enter the business is so high that sharing the investment is a prudent course of action. The European aircraft consortium, Airbus Industrie, is an example of such a joint venture.

A company may exit a business by both external and internal means. The external route is termed a *divestiture* (upper right block). An acquisition and a divestiture may be viewed as opposite sides of the same coin. For every buyer, there must be a seller on the other side of the table. In fact, I believe that the most proficient practitioners of the craft of Corporate Development are those who have set on both sides of this table at one time or another.

The final combination is exiting a business via internal means (lower right block), which is called *shutting down*, winding down or harvesting the business. If a company has made a definite decision to get out of a business, the preferred route is usually to try to find a buyer for the business. When this is not feasible, the only alternative is to shut the business down with minimal expense and residual obligations. This task is sometimes assumed by the Corporate Development executive, especially when the motivations of the General Manager of the business that is being shut down conflict with the corporate objective of shutting it down.

Figure 11-1
The Corporate Development Matrix

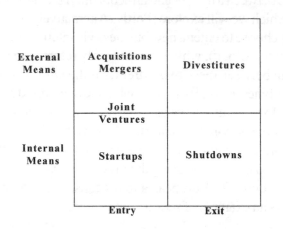

In any event, whether a company is entering or exiting a business by external or internal means, there is a paramount need for a thorough strategic plan for the business and reliable long-range financial projections. If the deal is an acquisition, the financials are mandatory to determine a reasonable purchase price. Conversely, if it is a divestiture, they are needed to peg a reasonable selling price. For a startup, the strategic plan is essential to ascertain the capital required to fund the startup. And for shutdowns, one needs to see whether winding the business down will generate or consume funds, and how much.

There are trade-offs involved in addressing the question of whether to pursue internal or external means for entering and exiting businesses. In the entry mode, the trade-off between acquisition (external) and startup (internal) involves such issues as:

Plan For Profitability!

- The comparative cost of entry between acquiring a business and starting one from scratch.

- The availability of acquisition candidates.

- The speed with which the company desires to enter the new business. Acquiring a going concern is usually quicker than starting up one.

- The availability of internal resources for startup. Some times a company will simply not have the know-how to start up a new business.

- The company's ability to integrate an acquisition. Acquisitions that fail do so more often than not because of culture clashes.

- Any negative features of the acquisition candidate.

The trade-off between divesting a business and shutting it down entails comparable considerations:

- The comparative return between divesting the business and shutting it down.

- The availability of candidate buyers for the business.

- The speed with which the company wants to get rid of the business.

I mentioned earlier that the Corporate Development executive has to be able to keep several balls in the air at the same time. Over the five-year time frame from 1979 to

1984, I was Vice President of Corporate Planning and Development for Storage Technology Corporation, a manufacturer of mainframe computer peripherals with annual revenues in excess of $1 billion. In addition to setting up and orchestrating the company's strategic planning system, I also led and coordinated 23 different Corporate Development projects during the same time frame, as follows:

Mergers and Acquisitions:	10
Divestitures:	7
Startups:	4
Shutdowns:	2

Clearly, I had several projects underway at any one time, in addition to my planning activities. I hasten to add that not all of the projects were successful, but such is the batting average that comes with the job.

SECONDARY VALUATION TECHNIQUES

The fundamental question in buying or selling a business is: how much is it worth? There are several ways that one can address this question and it is usually informative to employ several of them to arrive at a spread of valuations. The right answer will usually lie somewhere between the minimum and maximum extremes of the spread.

The ultimate answer is that price that is agreed upon between the buyer and the seller, with the seller seeking to maximize the price and the buyer trying for as low a price as possible. Before entering into negotiations, the prudent buyer does his homework and establishes a target price and a ceiling above which he will not go. Likewise the seller establishes his price and a floor below which he will not go. Of course, neither the buyer nor the seller knows the other's range of reasonableness, but if it turns out in the course of negotiations that the two ranges overlap, then the deal is usually consummated.

There are four techniques that should be considered in establishing a value for a business. I view three of them as *secondary valuation techniques*. These secondary techniques are useful yardsticks in appraising a business, but they are not sufficient among themselves.

In no special order, the first secondary technique is the *book value* of the business. On the balance sheet, book value is the difference between assets and liabilities, i.e., the equity in the business. Most of the time, the true value of a business is greater than its book value. This is because most businesses have assets that are not properly reflected on the balance sheet. For example, real estate on the balance sheet is valued at cost less accumulated depreciation. If real estate assets have been on the books for a period of time, their true market value may have appreciated substantially and not be reflected in their book value. Another example of undervalued assets are intangible assets such as proprietary technology. The value assigned to patents for such technology may reflect only a fraction of their real worth.

On the other hand, there are circumstances where book value overstates the value of a business. Older businesses sometimes have a substantial portion of their inventory that is obsolete or turns very slowly and needs to be written down. Intangible assets such as goodwill (discussed later in this chapter) sometimes bloat the assets side of the balance sheet.

If the company is publicly traded, another secondary valuation benchmark is the *market value* of the company's shares. This is simply the per share price of the company's shares multiplied by the number of outstanding shares. Market value also represents a floor on the company's true value, since shareholders are unlikely to sell their holdings to an acquiring company for less than the shares will fetch on the open market. Deals are usually consummated at a differential above the company's market value, which is called the *premium*.

Another secondary benchmark is the *price-to-earnings (P/E)* approach. This approach is particularly useful if a company is not publicly traded. You may recall that we discussed the concept of earnings per share (EPS) back in Chapter VIII. The price-to-earnings multiple of a publicly traded company is given by:

$$P/E = \frac{Share\ Price}{EPS}$$

In other words, P/E is simply the multiple of earnings at which a company's shares trade. In valuing a privately held company, the approach is to identify publicly traded companies that are in the same industry as the target company and to determine their price-to-earnings ratios. It may be possible to arrive at a P/E that is representative of the industry in which the target company participates. Then the target company's value would be:

Value = (Industry P/E) x (Target Company EPS)

THE CONCEPT OF NET PRESENT VALUE

The foregoing three techniques, book value, market value

and P/E, yield estimates of the value of a business. In some cases, the valuation may represent a floor below which the actual value cannot exist; in other cases, a ceiling; and sometimes neither. In short, all three approaches yield results that are in the ballpark, but subject to some latitude in their interpretation.

The best approach to valuing a business is to determine its *net present value*. This is simply the present value of the cash flow that the business is projected to generate in the future. To the extent that the strategic plan for the business is thoughtfully prepared and the financial projections represent the most reasonable forecast, determining the present value of the stream of cash flow that the business produces is by far the most accurate gauge of the value of the business.

Most of you are probably familiar with the concept of the present value of money, but for those who are not, here is a short tutorial. The concept is that a sum of money today is worth more than the same sum at some point in the future. The reasoning is that the sum of money today can be invested today at the prevailing interest rate and will be worth more at the future point. For example, if the prevailing interest rate is 10%, $100 today can be compounded into $110 a year from now.

Or from the other point of view, $100 a year from now is worth only $90.91 today, since the interest on $90.91 at 10% is $9.09. The amount of $90.91 is called the *present value* of $100.00 a year from now at a *discount rate* of 10%.

Though the concept is straightforward, there are three issues that must be addressed before we can put the concept into practice. These are:

1) What is the cash flow of a business?

2) Since most strategic plans have a planning horizon of five years or less, how does one account for cash generated beyond the last year of the plan?

3) What discount rate should be employed?

To the first question, many people have difficulty grasping the concept of the cash flow of a business. My approach to comprehending and explaining cash flow may not appeal to a CPA, but it works for me and may also for you. In short, any change in the financial statements of a company that increases cash on the balance sheet produces positive cash flow. If the change decreases cash on the balance sheet, the cash flow is negative. The simplified balance sheet of Figure 11-2 helps me to envision this concept.

Figure 11-2
Simplified Balance Sheet

Cash		Total Liabilities
+ All Non-Cash Assets		+ Shares Outstanding
- Depreciation		+ Retained Earnings
Total Assets	=	Liabilities and Equity

A balance sheet is called that because it must balance, i.e., assets must equal the sum of liabilities and shareholders' equity. For example, an increase in liabilities (to the exclusion of any other changes) results in an increase in the right-hand side of the balance sheet; so also must the left-hand side (assets) increase, which results in an increase in cash. It follows that there are five categories of changes that produce positive cash flow:

> 1) An increase in retained earnings (the generation of net income)
> 2) An increase in accumulated depreciation
> 3) An increase in liabilities (e.g., accounts payable, debt, etc.)
> 4) A decrease in non-cash assets (e.g., inventory, accounts receivable, etc.)
> 5) An increase in the number of outstanding shares

Cash flow, therefore, can be expressed as:

> Cash flow = Net income
> + Depreciation
> + Increases in liabilities
> + Decreases in non-cash assets
> + Sales of shares

If you are skeptical of this simplistic explanation of cash flow, go back to Chapter VIII, specifically to Figures 8-4 (the operating statement), 8-5 (the balance sheet) and 8-6 (the funds flow statement). Calculate the net income and the changes to the balance sheet from one year to the next according to the foregoing formula and verify that they amount to the changes in cash from the cash flow statement.

To the second question that we posed, since most strategic plans have a planning horizon of five years or less, how does one account for cash generated beyond the last year of the plan? To do so, we have to make some assumptions about the cash flow beyond the fifth year of the plan. This should not cause too much concern because (1) forecasting accuracy that far out is questionable and (2) the effect of cash flow generated beyond the fifth year falls off rapidly because of the compounding effect and the relatively high discount rates that are usually employed in the calculation of net present value. For example, putting aside the reason for the high discount rates for just a moment, at a discount rate of 20%, $1.00 of cash flow in the sixth year contributes only $0.40 of net present value (NPV). The same $1.00 in the tenth year produces only $0.19 of NPV.

Moreover, the planner's ability to project cash flow accurately beyond, say, five years must also be called into question. With these points in mind, my approach is to forecast cash flow as accurately as I can for at least five years and then to assume that the cash flow in the fifth year of the forecast repeats itself in the sixth and subsequent years of the stream until such time that the incremental addition to NPV is minimal. This technique can easily be accommodated with spreadsheet programs.

To the final question: what discount rate should be employed? Most companies establish what is called a *hurdle rate* (sometimes also referred to as the internal rate of return or IRR) in evaluating potential acquisitions. The concept is that the price of the acquisition cannot be higher than that which will clear the company's hurdle rate of return. In other words, the net present value of the cash flow stream generated with a discount rate equal to the company's hurdle rate fixes the maximum price that the company should pay for the acquisition.

There are two popular approaches to determining the hurdle rate of an acquiring company. One is to set the rate at a value equal to or greater than the return on investment (ROI) of the company. (See Chapter IX for a review of the concept of the ROI of a business.) In this manner, the ROI of the acquiring company will not be deteriorated by the absorption of the acquired company.

Another approach is to quantify the return of a risk-free investment and then to add a premium to the risk-free return to address the fact that the acquisition of a company is scarcely a risk-free investment. U.S. treasury bills are generally viewed as a risk-free standard. If treasury bills are returning 8% per annum, for example, one might add another 8% risk premium to arrive at a hurdle rate of 16%. In my experience, I have seen hurdle rates from as low as 12% to as high as 25%.

Figure 11-3 presents the cash flow and NPV calculation for a semiconductor plant that I divested in 1984. We were asking $22.5 million for the plant. Using the ground rules that I just discussed, this equated to an internal rate of return of 20.7%.

Figure 11-3
Cash Flow and Net Present Value
for a Semiconductor Plant
($ in thousands)

	Year 1	Year 2	Year 3	Year 4	Year 5
Revenues	29,201	41,715	50,058	58,401	66,744
Net Income	(2,042)	519	2,265	4,182	6,041
Depreciation	2,561	2,861	3,161	3,461	3,761
Capital Equipment	(1,500)	(1,500)	(1,500)	(1,500)	(1,500)
Inventory	(4,106)	(1,107)	(1,838)	616	529
Accounts Receivable	(3,650)	(1,538)	(1,069)	(1,025)	(1,056)
Accounts Payable	8,193	2,014	2,602	(180)	(67)
Cash Flow	(544)	1,249	3,621	5,554	7,708

Asking Price: 22,500
Internal Rate of Return: 20.7%

MERGERS VERSUS ACQUISITIONS

When two companies decide to combine, there may be two possible forms of combination, *merger* or *acquisition*. The conceptual difference between the two may be illustrated by a graphical example. Consider two companies, which we shall call Goliath and David. Figure 11-4 depicts the revenue stream of Goliath over seven years, which are labeled Years 1 through 7 for simplicity. Note that the revenues of Goliath increase from $10 million to $22 million over the time period.

Figure 11-4
Goliath
($ in millions)

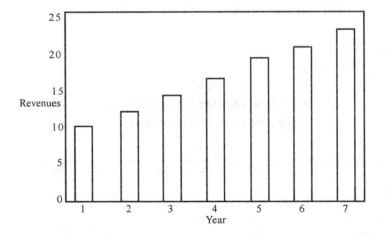

Figure 11-5 displays the revenue stream for David over the same time frame. Observe that the revenues of David increase from $2 million to $14 million over the same period.

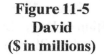

Figure 11-5
David
($ in millions)

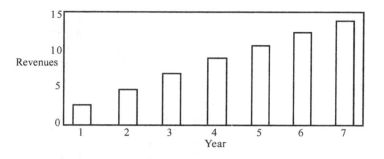

Now suppose that the two companies decide to combine at the beginning of Year 4. Assume first that the combination takes the form of an acquisition. In an acquisition, one company purchases another; hence, the terms *acquisition* and *purchase* are used interchangeably. If Goliath is the acquiring company and David the acquired company, then the revenue stream of the acquiring company, Goliath, would be that shown in Figure 11-6. Notice that there is no acknowledgment of the existence of David as a company prior to the acquisition, nor of its revenue stream.

On the other hand, suppose that instead of an acquisition, the two companies decided to merge. The term *merger* is synonymous with a *pooling of interests*. The financial statements of the combined companies reflect the existence of both companies prior to the merger. The financial statements are recast retrospectively as if the companies had been combined prior to the merger. This is reflected in Figure 11-7, where the revenues of both Goliath and David are recognized prior to the merger as well as after it.

Figure 11-6
Acquisition of David by Goliath
($ in millions)

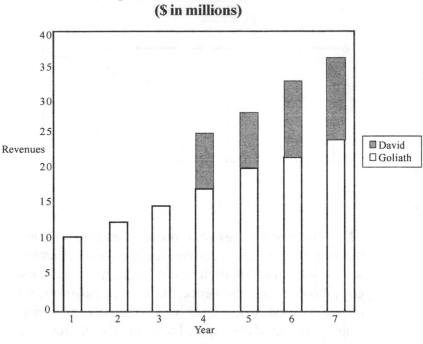

GOODWILL

There are pros and cons to both forms of business combination. One of the problems with the acquisition alternative is the possibility that the acquiring company may have to reflect a portion of the purchase price as an intangible asset known as *goodwill*. In fundamental terms, goodwill is the difference between the purchase price for a company and its book value. You may recall that, earlier in this chapter, we talked about book value as one of the yardsticks of the value of a company. At that time, I observed that most companies are intrinsically worth more than their book value because of intangible assets and even tangible assets that are undervalued on the balance sheet.

Figure 11-7
Merger of Goliath and David
($ in millions)

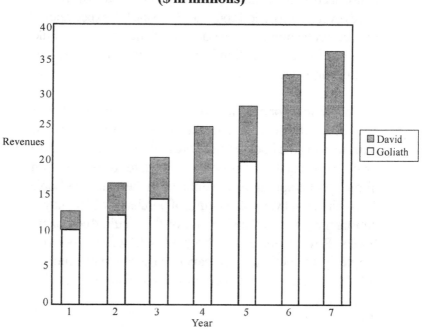

To illustrate this concept, suppose that the book value of David at the end of Year 3 was $10 million and that the two companies struck a deal whereby Goliath would acquire (purchase) David for the sum of $15 million. Goliath would add $10 million of assets to its balance sheet to reflect the net assets of David and, in return, Goliath would subtract $15 million from its assets to compensate the shareholders of David. The difference of $5 million would appear on the balance sheet of Goliath as goodwill, as follows:

Purchase price:	$15 million
Less book value:	10 million
Goodwill:	$ 5 million

The problem with goodwill is that it generally hangs around on the acquiring company's balance sheet for a long time because accounting rules require that it be written off (amortized) over a long period comparable to the life expectancy of the acquired company. To compound the situation, unlike depreciation, amortization is not recognized as an expense for tax purposes.

To minimize or even avoid goodwill, an acquiring company generally tries to revalue the assets of the acquired company to bring the book value more in line with the purchase price. Real estate is a primary candidate for revaluation. Typically, it is appraised and entered on the acquirer's books at its fair market value at the time of purchase, which may be substantially greater than its value on the acquired company's books. Revaluation can cut both ways, however. As an example, it is sometimes necessary to write down inventory to reflect obsolete stock, which only exacerbates the problem of goodwill.

A merger, also called a pooling of interests, avoids the issue of goodwill. There are some rather strict criteria that must be fulfilled for two companies to be able to qualify for a pooling of interests. While the detailed requirements are beyond the scope of this book, suffice it to say that two of the important criteria are that (1) the two companies must have maintained an arm's length relationship for at least two years prior to the deal and (2) the surviving company must issue common stock for the assets of the acquired company (or for 90% of the common shares of the acquired company).

DILUTION

Thus, mergers are stock deals and avoid goodwill. However, there can be other problems. To illustrate this, suppose that Goliath and David decide to do their deal as a merger rather than an acquisition. To proceed, we need some more information about the two companies just prior to their combination (at the end of Year 3). This is summarized in Figure 11-8.

Notice first from this exhibit that both the P/E's of the two companies are identical at 20 times earnings. This is admittedly contrived for the purpose of this example, but one would expect to find the P/E's of two companies in the same industry to be comparable. Observe also that the market value of David's shares (the number of shares outstanding times the market price per share) is $12 million. We now have three benchmarks for the value of David:

Purchase price:	$15 million
Market value:	12 million
Book value:	10 million

Figure 11-8
David and Goliath before the Merger

	Goliath	David
Revenues ($ in thousands)	14,000	6,000
Net Income ($ in thousands)	1,000	600
Return on Sales (ROS)	7.1%	10.0%
Shares Outstanding	400,000	600,000
Earnings per Share (EPS) ($)	2.50	1.00
Price-to-Earnings (P/E)	20	20
Share Price ($)	50.00	20.00
Market Value ($ in thousands)	20,000	12,000

Relative to market value, the premium that Goliath planned to offer the shareholders of David in the purchase scenario was:

$$\text{Premium} = \frac{\$15 \text{ million} - \$12 \text{ million}}{\$12 \text{ million}} = 25\%$$

In other words, for each $20 share of David, the shareholders were going to receive $25. Few shareholders would pass up the chance for an immediate 25% return on their investment.

In the stock swap, Goliath proposes to exchange one of its shares (value = $50) for every two shares of David (value = $40). This is called a 1-for-2 stock exchange. It superficially appears to accomplish the same goal of paying a 25% premium to the shareholders of David. But does it really?

Figure 11-9 displays what actually would result. Both the revenues and net income of the two companies would simply be added together. The resulting ROS of the combined company would become 8%. The number of shares outstanding would increase by 300,000 (half of 600,000) from 400,000 to 700,000. EPS for the combined company would amount to $2.29.

One can never predict with certainty how the market would react, but a rational supposition would be that the price-to-earnings multiple of the combined company would remain in the regime of that of the two separate companies at 20x earnings. That being the case, the share price of the new company would be $45.71.

There are two groups of losers in this scenario. The shareholders of David receive only $45.71 for each two shares of the company, not $50.00 as originally intended. Instead of a premium of 25%, their premium is only 14.3%. The shareholders of Goliath also lose. They experience a drop in their per-share price from $50.00 to $45.71 as a result of the merger, a loss of 8.6%.

Figure 11-9
David and Goliath after the Merger
(1-for-2 exchange)

	Goliath	David	Combined
Revenues ($ in thousands)	14,000	6,000	20,000
Net Income ($ in thousands)	1,000	600	1,600
Return on Sales (ROS)	7.1%	10.0%	8.0%
Shares Outstanding	400,000	600,000	700,000
Earnings per Share (EPS) ($)	2.50	1.00	2.29
Price-to-Earnings (P/E)	20	20	20
Share Price ($)	50.00	20.00	45.71
Market Value ($ in thousands)	20,000	12,000	32,000

This latter phenomenon is called *dilution*. The new shares are said to have diluted the old shares because the per-share earnings that accompanied the new shares were less than the per-share earnings of the company before the merger. Dilution occurs whenever a company exchanges its shares for those of another company at a price that translates into a P/E that is greater than the P/E of its shares. In this case, Goliath wants to compensate the shareholders of David at $25.00 per share. Since the EPS of David is $1.00, Goliath is paying a multiple of 25 times earnings, which is more than its own multiple of 20 times. Ergo, dilution.

Of course, one could structure the deal such that the shareholders of David receive the 25% premium that was intended. This scenario is summarized in Figure 11-10. Instead of two shares, if the shareholders of David surrender only 1.7 shares (valued at $34.00) in return for one share of Goliath (valued at $42.50), they will receive their 25% premium. Unfortunately, the shareholders of Goliath will suffer even more dilution.

Figure 11-10
David and Goliath after the Merger
(1-for-1.7 exchange)

	Goliath	David	Combined
Revenues ($ in thousands)	14,000	6,000	20,000
Net Income ($ in thousands)	1,000	600	1,600
Return on Sales (ROS)	7.1%	10.0%	8.0%
Shares Outstanding	400,000	600,000	753,000
Earnings per Share (EPS) ($)	2.50	1.00	2.12
Price-to-Earnings (P/E)	20	20	20
Share Price ($)	50.00	20.00	42.50
Market Value ($ in thousands)	20,000	12,000	32,000

To avoid dilution, the P/E of the company with the surviving shares needs to be greater than the P/E paid for the exchanged shares, i.e., the price paid for the exchanged shares divided by the number of shares exchanged. For this reason, active merger seekers usually have high price-to-earnings multiples on their stock. Figure 11-11 is an alternative scenario for our merger where the P/E for David is sufficiently lower than that of Goliath that, even with the 25% premium, the P/E tendered for the shares of David does not exceed that of Goliath. Note that the shareholders of David receive their full 25% premium and the shareholders of Goliath do not suffer any dilution.

Plan For Profitability!

Figure 11-11
Alternative Scenario for David and Goliath
(1-for-2.5 exchange)

	Goliath	David	Combined
Revenues ($ in thousands)	14,000	6,000	20,000
Net Income ($ in thousands)	1,000	600	1,600
Return on Sales (ROS)	7.1%	10.0%	8.0%
Shares Outstanding	400,000	600,000	640,000
Earnings per Share (EPS) ($)	2.50	1.00	2.50
Price-to-Earnings (P/E)	20	16	20
Share Price ($)	50.00	16.00	50.00
Market Value ($ in thousands)	20,000	9,600	32,000

THE ACQUISITION OF GENERAL WIDGETS

When we left International Microwidgets in Chapter IX, the only open item was the acquisition of General Widgets. As mentioned previously, the financial performance of General Widgets has been in decline for years. Market share has steadily eroded and revenues have declined to the point where the company has turned a profit in only two of the past five years. Figure 11-12 presents a summary of the company's operating performance for the current year and the preceding two.

Figure 11-12
General Widgets Operating History

Year	-2(A)	-1(A)	0(E)
Revenues ($ in millions)	115	110	100
Net Income ($ in millions)	1.0	-0.2	-0.5
Return on Sales (ROS)	0.9%	-0.2%	-0.5%
Earnings per Share (EPS) ($)	0.20	-0.04	-0.10
Price-to-Earnings (P/E)	25	NA	NA
Shares Outstanding	5,000,000	5,000,000	5,000,000
Share Price ($)	5.00	5.00	5.00
Market Value ($ in millions)	25	25	25

As can be seen from the table, the revenues of General Widgets have fallen to $100 million, $80 million of which are generated from the U.S./Canada region and the rest from Latin America. The company was in the red last year (Year -1) and is projected to have another loss in the current year. Its share price has bottomed out at $5.00, which is comparable to the company's book value per share. Clearly, prospects for General Widgets and its customers, employees and shareholders are not upbeat.

In discussions with the CEO of General Widgets, Bill Portes has arrived at an agreement in principle to acquire General Widgets via an exchange of stock. (To be precise, this is a merger, not an acquisition.) The parameters that have been tentatively established are based on an 8:1 exchange: each shareholder of General Widgets will receive one share of International Microwidgets for eight shares of General Widgets. In all, five million shares of General Widgets will be swapped for 625,000 shares of International Microwidgets.

The deal needs to be approved by the Boards of Directors of both companies and then by the shareholders. Subject to these approvals, Portes and the CEO of General Widgets have set the target date for the merger at July 1st of the coming year.

Figure 11-13 is Portes's operating forecast for the first year of the merger (Year 1). Note that he projects a further decline in the revenues of General Widgets from $100 million this year to $90 million next year. However, Portes believes that, if he moves quickly to consolidate the operations of General Widgets with those of his company and eliminate redundant expenses, he can reduce losses for the year to a nominal amount.

Figure 11-13
Merger of International Microwidgets
and General Widgets
Year 1 Operating Forecast

	International	General	Combined
Revenues ($ in millions)	880	90	970
Net Income ($ in millions)	29	0	29
Return on Sales (ROS)	3.3%	0.0%	3.0%
Shares Outstanding	17,575,000	5,000,000	18,200,000
Earnings per Share (EPS) ($)	1.65	Nil	1.59
Price-to-Earnings (P/E)	24	NA	25
Share Price ($)	40.00	5.00	40.00
Market Value ($ in millions)	703	25	728

The best acquisitions or mergers are those that are win-win situations: both sides come away with something better than they had before. It helps to look at this deal from both sides. From the viewpoint of General Widgets, its stakeholders are exchanging a future of inevitably declining prospects for an association with the market leader and the attendant prospects for growth.

To the question of value received for the shareholders of General Widgets, their shares have been stagnant at $5.00 per share for several years and prospects for appreciation are negligible. Since the amount of International Microwidgets shares to be issued (625,000) is small in comparison with the total number of shares outstanding (17,575,000), dilution will be small. Hence, the share price of International Microwidgets after the deal can be expected to be comparable to that before the deal.

Assuming a price of $40.00 per share at the time of the merger, a swap of eight shares of General Widgets at $5.00 per share for one share of International Microwidgets is clearly just a breakeven transaction in the short term for the shareholders of General Widgets. In the long run, however, both CEO's believe that prospect of trading in shares with little potential for appreciation for those with significant upside potential will be attractive to the shareholders of General Widgets.

From the viewpoint of International Microwidgets, the merger will boost annual revenues by $90 million and increase the company's market share to 68% in the U.S./Canada region and 78% in Latin America. (See Figure 4-10.) Unfortunately, these increased revenues carry with them the near-term penalty of zero profit. As a result, ROS in the year of the merger is projected to drop from 3.3% to 3.0%.

The long-term view is more sanguine. Under the aegis of International Microwidgets, the additional revenue stream of General Widgets should generate profit as soon as the efficiencies of the merger are realized. If one assumes an ROS of 5% (the average ROS of International Microwidgets over the six-year period of Figure 8-7), then $90 million in revenues yields $4.5 million of net income. Giving up $5 million in equity for $4.5 million of earnings corresponds to a price-to-earnings (P/E) multiple of 1.1. In other words, the future earnings potential of the revenues of General Widgets is roughly the same as the purchase price. This is definitely a good deal for the shareholders of International Microwidgets!

SUMMARY

Corporate Development encompasses those projects that are company-wide in scope and do not logically fall under the purview of one of the business or functional units of the company. Included in this category are mergers, acquisitions, joint ventures, startups, divestitures and shutdowns. Here are some points to remember:

- In an acquisition, the acquiring company purchases the acquired company. After the acquisition, the financial performance of the acquired company prior to the deal is not reflected in the acquired company's historical financials.

- In a merger, the two companies pool their interests. Historical financials are presented as if the two companies had been combined prior to the date of their merger.

- Three useful, albeit secondary, valuation techniques are the book value, the market value and the P/E approach.

- The primary approach in valuing a company is to ascertain the net present value (NPV) of its cash flow. In this approach, future cash flow is discounted on a compound interest basis by a discount rate, also called the internal rate of return (IRR). Many companies have a minimum discount rate called the hurdle rate that they use in assessing deals.

- An acquisition may result in goodwill on the balance sheet of the acquiring company. Goodwill is the excess of the purchase price over the book value of the acquired company.

- Mergers are stock deals. Mergers may result in dilution of the shares of the acquiring company.

CHAPTER XII
THE STRATEGIC PLAN
OF INTERNATIONAL MICROWIDGETS

> I grow daily to honour facts more and more, and theory less and less. A fact, it seems to me, is a great thing.
> Thomas Carlyle, 1836
>
> All successful men have agreed in one thing: they were causationists. They believed that things went not by luck, but by law; that there was not a weak or a cracked link in the chain that joins the first and last of things.
> Ralph Waldo Emerson, 1860

Presented on the following pages is the Strategic Business Plan that the CEO of International Microwidgets, Bill Portes, presented to his Board of Directors. Note that is concise and to the point, consistent with the maxim of conveying information to executives as efficiently and succinctly as possible. In the event that the Directors want to explore any facet of the plan in more detail, Portes is amply fortified with backup material.

In presenting the Strategic Plan to Directors, my preference is to abridge my work to the following six condensed topics:

- Mission
- Market
- Competition
- My Company or SBU (Strengths, Weaknesses, Strategies and Goals)
- Resources
- Financials

Note in particular that the exhaustive analysis of the serial linkages between the internal/external environment and opportunities/threats, opportunities/threats and objectives, objectives and strategies, strategies and programs, and programs and goals is not presented. This objective of the linkage analysis is to ensure that the planner's logic is rational and flawless. In presentation to others, however, my experience is that the linkage charts tend to confuse the audience and that the essence of the linkage analysis is best conveyed by compressing it into a straightforward presentation of:

- The strengths and weaknesses of the company or SBU
- Strategies: What we intend to do to capitalize on our strengths and assuage our weaknesses
- Goals: When we intend to accomplish our actions

This is the approach taken by Bill Portes as he presents his Strategic Plan to the Board of Directors. Note that the entire plan is condensed to just a few pages.

MISSION

International Microwidgets is the largest and lowest-cost producer of microwidgets in the world. The company is universally recognized as the inventor of the microwidget and a pioneer in expanding the applications of microwidgets to diverse markets. The company intends to maintain its leadership by creatively continuing to improve the affordability of its products and by aggressively positioning its products as the products of choice throughout the world.

Plan For Profitability!

MARKET

The worldwide market for microwidgets is growing at 14% per year, with the fastest growth in Asia/Pacific and Eastern Europe. In this plan, all data is in current dollars, the assumed inflation rate is 3.5 % and dollar figures are in millions unless otherwise noted.

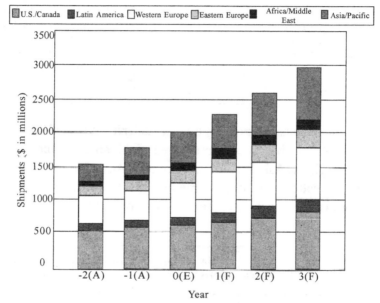

Year	-2(A)	-1(A)	0(E)	1(F)	2(F)	3 (F)	AAG
U.S./ Canada	500	540	600	660	720	800	10%
Latin America	100	120	140	160	180	200	15%
Western Europe	440	480	540	600	680	760	12%
Eastern Europe	120	160	180	220	260	300	20%
Africa/ Middle East	80	80	100	120	120	140	12%
Asia/ Pacific	300	360	440	520	640	760	20%
Total	**1540**	**1740**	**2000**	**2280**	**2600**	**2960**	**14%**

COMPETITION

International Microwidgets, Microwidgets Ichiban and Deutsche Microwidgets command 85% of the worldwide market. General Widgets is a distant fourth and its revenues are in decline.

Year	-2(A)	-1(A)	0(E)	AAG
International Microwidgets	580	680	800	17%
Microwidgets Ichiban	360	420	500	18%
Deutsche Microwidgets	285	330	400	18%
General Widgets	115	110	100	-7%
Others	200	200	200	0%
Total	**1540**	**1740**	**2000**	**14%**

International Microwidgets is the leader in the United States/ Canada and the Latin America areas, Ichiban dominates the market in the Asia/Pacific region, and Deutsche Microwidgets is the leader in the other three areas. The following table portrays the competitive scenario by geographical area in the current year.

	U.S./ Canada	Latin America	Western Europe	Easterm Europe	Africa/ M. East	Asia/ Pacific	Total
International Microwidgets	400	90	160	40	20	90	800
Widgets Ichiban	170	20	50	10	30	220	500
Deutsche Microwidgets	20	10	230	80	50	10	400
General Widgets	80	20	--	--	--	--	100
Others	30	--	80	10	--	80	200
Total	**700**	**140**	**520**	**140**	**100**	**400**	**2000**

Plan For Profitability!

Microwidgets Ichiban

Strengths	Weaknesses
● Low cost of manufacture, with a captive source of semiconductor components ● Image as an innovator ● Leading market share in the Asia/Pacific region (55%) ● Second leading market share in the United States/Canada region (24%)	● Less significant market share in the other four regions of the world (12%) ● Exports into major markets hampered by Japan's trade surpluses and the strong yen

Probable Strategies

● Focus top priority on dominating the emerging markets in the Asia/Pacific region

● Continue to drive down manufacturing costs with accumulated volume coupled with value engineering

● Compete in the other markets of the world by reducing profit margins where feasible

Deutsche Microwidgets

Strengths	Weaknesses
● Image as a quality product ● Leading market share in the Western Europe region (44%) ● Leading market share in the rapidly growing Eastern Europe region (57%) and in the Africa/Middle East region (50%)	● High selling prices due to high cost of manufacture ● Negligible presence in the United States/Canada and Asia/Pacific regions (3%)

Probable Strategies

● Concentrate exports on those regions of traditional strength for European companies: Eastern Europe and Africa/Middle East

● Pursue other regions opportunistically be promoting the superior quality of the product line

● Reduce manufacturing costs as feasible through increased volumes

295

General Widgets

Strength	Weakness
● A substantial customer base in the United States/Canada and Latin America regions	● Precarious financial position
Probable Strategies	
● Continue to look for a rescuer ● Failing that, consider protection under the bankruptcy laws	

INTERNATIONAL MICROWIDGETS

Strengths	Weaknesses
● Recognized as the pioneer of the modern microwidget ● Leading share of the worldwide market (40%) ● Lowest-cost manufacturer in the market ● Strong financial position	● Declining improvement in product margins ● Distant second-place share in the Asia/Pacific region (20%) ● Distant second-place share in the Eastern Europe region (29%)

Strategies	Goals
Acquire General Widgets	Close the acquisition by the middle of Year 1
Manufacture microchips internally	Begin internal microchip manufacture by the end of Year 1
Assemble in the Asia/Pacific region	Begin assembly in China by the end of Year 1
Assemble in Eastern Europe	Begin assembly in Eastern Europe by the end of Year 1

RESOURCES

The addition of the two assembly plants and the microchip manufacturing plant will require an additional $200 million in property, plant and equipment in the coming year.

Plan For Profitability!

New PP&E Year	-2(A)	-1(A)	0(E)	1(F)	2(F)	3(F)
Property	0	0	0	10	0	0
Plant	0	0	0	100	0	0
Equipment	50	60	70	150	80	90
Total ($ millions)	50	60	70	260	80	90

Headcount outside of U.S./Canada will increase by almost 1000 employees over the next two years to staff the plants in China and Eastern Europe. To keep domestic headcount level, personnel will be transferred from domestic assembly plants to the new microchip plant. Revenues/Employee will plateau temporarily as new employees attain requisite productivity.

Employees Year	-2(A)	-1(A)	0(E)	1(F)	2(F)	3(F)
U.S./Canada	2600	2875	3240	3200	3200	3400
Rest of the World	300	325	360	600	1300	1500
Total	2900	3200	3600	3800	4500	4900
Revenues/Employee ($000)	200	213	222	232	231	247

Facility Space/Employee will increase temporarily next year as the new plants are completed but the full complement of employees to staff them has not been reached.

Facility Space (sq. feet)	-2(A)	-1(A)	0(E)	1(F)	2(F)	3(F)
U.S./Canada	655	720	810	800	800	875
Rest of the World	70	80	90	310	325	350
Total	725	800	900	1110	1125	1225
Facility Space/ Employee	250	250	250	292	250	250

Total expenses as a percent of revenues will be contained over the planning horizon.

Expenses Year	-2(A)	-1(A)	0(E)	1(F)	2(F)	3(F)
Marketing	145	170	200	220	255	300
Engineering	70	80	95	105	125	145
G&A	45	55	65	70	85	100
Total ($ millions)	260	305	360	395	465	545
Expenses/Revenues	45%	45%	45%	45%	45%	45%

FINANCIALS

The decline in gross margin will be reversed in Year 2 as the cost savings of manufacturing our own microchips and assembling products offshore are realized. By Year 3, gross margin is projected to be at its highest level in six years.

The current plan is to fund the additional $200 million of PP&E by debt. The debt service forecast is predicated upon borrowing at 8% and retiring the debt at $10 million per year.

The combined effect of interest on this debt and declining gross margin will result in a one-time adverse impact on earnings next year. Net income, which has been stagnant at $40 million per year for three years, is projected to drop to $29 million. Likewise, earnings per share are forecast to tumble from a three-year plateau of $2.30 to $1.65.

This transient deterioration of earnings will be reversed in the Year 2 as margin improvement more than offsets debt service. By Year 3, per-share earnings are expected to be at a level almost twice that of their current plateau.

Operating Statement

Year	-2(A)	-1(A)	0(E)	1(F)	2(F)	3(F)
Revenues	580	680	800	880	1040	1210
Cost of Revenues	230	280	340	380	430	470
Gross Profit	350	400	460	500	610	740
Gross Margin	60%	59%	58%	57%	59%	61%
Marketing	145	170	200	220	255	300
Engineering	70	80	95	105	125	145
General and Administrative	45	55	65	70	85	100
Total Expenses	260	305	360	395	465	545
Operating Profit	90	95	100	105	145	195
Interest	0	0	0	16	15	14
Depreciation	30	35	40	45	50	60
Interest & Depreciation	30	35	40	61	65	74
Pre-Tax Income	60	60	60	44	80	121
Taxes	20	20	20	15	30	45
Net Income	40	40	40	29	50	76
Net Income/Revenue	7%	6%	5%	3%	5%	6%
Earning Per Share ($)	2.31	2.30	2.29	1.65	2.81	4.25

Balance Sheet

Year	-2(A)	-1(A)	0(E)	1(F)	2(F)	3(F)
Cash and Equivalents	115	110	94	94	71	75
Accounts Receivable	97	113	133	147	173	202
Inventory	193	227	267	293	347	403
Current Assets	**405**	**450**	**494**	**534**	**591**	**680**
PP&E	600	660	730	990	1070	1160
Less Depreciation	400	435	475	520	570	630
Fixed Assets	**200**	**225**	**255**	**470**	**500**	**530**
Total Assets	**605**	**675**	**749**	**1004**	**1091**	**1210**
Accounts Payable	116	136	160	176	208	242
Current Long-Term Debt	0	0	0	10	10	10
Taxes Payable		5	5	5	5	10
15						
Current Liabilities	**121**	**141**	**165**	**191**	**228**	**267**
Long-Term Debt	0	0	0	190	180	170
Total Liabilities	**121**	**141**	**165**	**381**	**408**	**437**
Paid-In Capital	100	105	110	115	120	125
Retained Earnings	500	540	580	620	649	699
Shareholders' Equity	**600**	**645**	**690**	**735**	**769**	**824**
Total Liabilities & Equity	721	786	855	1116	1177	1261

Sources And Uses Of Funds

Net Income	40	40	40	29	50	76
Depreciation	30	35	40	45	50	60
Accounts Payable	15	20	24	16	32	34
Deferred Taxes	5	5	5	5	10	15
Paid-In Capital	5	5	5	5	5	5
Long-Term Debt	0	0	0	200	0	0
Total Sources of Cash	**95**	**105**	**114**	**300**	**147**	**190**
Accounts Receivable	15	17	20	13	27	28
Inventory	40	33	40	27	53	57
PP&E	50	60	70	260	80	90
Repayment of Debt	0	0	0	0	10	10
Total Uses of Cash	**105**	**110**	**130**	**300**	**170**	**185**
Cash Increase (Decrease)	**(10)**	**(5)**	**(16)**	**0**	**(29)**	**5**

INDEX

(A).................................... .... *See* Actual data
(E)................................*See* Estimated data
(F).. *See* Forecast data

A

AAG...................... *See* Average Annual Growth
Accounts payable 204
Accounts receivable.................................... 202
Acquisition 265
Actual data 60
Advanced Pumping Systems
    Goals 152
    Mission.. 35
    Objectives.................................. 147
    Opportunities and Threats 145
    Programs 150
    Strategies 148
AEG-Telefunken 11
Ain't We Got Fun 220
Airbus Industrie 265
Alarm patterns in forecasts 235
American Motors.. 82
AMF 93
Annual Planning Cycle
    Defined 22
    Flow chart 24
    Four steps of the cycle 22
    Operational Plan 22
    Strategic Plan 22
Arthur Andersen 1
Arthur D. Little.. 9
Average Annual Growth 56

B

Balance sheet
    Defined 169
    Industrial Terminal Systems........................ 201
    Interactions with the operating statement .. 192

International Microwidgets 211, 300
    Plugs 201
    Simplified 272
Baughn, William 6
Book value 269
Booz Allen and Hamilton 64, 82
Boston Consulting Group
    Learning curve 116
    Portfolio matrix 120
Bottom-up planning 246
Boulder, Colorado 18
Budget 248
Burke, Edmund 20, 244
Burns, Robert 108
Burroughs 16
Business Development
Development.......................................*See* Corporate
Business-oriented organization 254
Bytes 69

C

Capital equipment 169
Carlyle, Thomas 291
Carnegie, Andrew 76
Carroll, Lewis 20, 244
Cash cows 122
Cash flow 273
CASI ... *See* Computer Applications Systems Inc.
CASI-RUSCO
    Budget 248
    Operational Plan 248
    The author and .... 246, i
Castro, Fidel 1
Catholic University i
Causal variables 66
CEO ....*See* Chief Executive Officer
CGR .... *See* Compound Growth Rate
Chandler, Alfred 251
Chief Executive Officer
    Commitment to the Strategic Plan 20
    Responsibility for the Strategic Plan 12

Versus Chief Operating Officer 260
Chief Operating Officer 260
Chrysler 82
Common stock 206
Competition
    International Microwidgets 94, 294
    Role in the flow of the Strategic Plan 28
    Strengths and Weaknesses 87
Competitive data *See* Sources of competitive data
Competitive intelligence 83
Compound Growth Rate 56
Computer Applications Systems Inc. 247
Computer Automation i
Consolidating the environment 106
Constant dollars 54
Control Data 16
Controllable environment 106
COO .... *See* Chief Operating Officer
Coolidge, Calvin 183
Corporate Development 260, 264
Corporate Development matrix 266
Cost of goods sold 193
Creeping hockey stick 236
Crotonville, New York 5
Current assets 204
Current dollars 54
Current liabilities 206

D

D/E .... *See* Debt-to-equity ratio
Dataquest 72
Days payables 205, 231
Days receivables 202, 231
de Mille, Cecil B. 133
Debt
    Defined 224
    Versus equity 227
Debt-to-equity ratio 223
Depreciation 204
DeSoto 82
Deutsche Microwidgets

Market share 94
Strategies 101, 295
Strengths and Weaknesses 100, 295
Discount rate 271
Discretionary expenses 218, 231
Divestiture 265
Dogs 122
Dumont Laboratories 76

E

Earnings per share 200, 221
Econometric modeling 68
Eisenhower, Dwight D. 20
Elasticities 67
Emerson, Ralph Waldo 215, 291
Engineering expense 232
ENIAC 16
Environment .... *See* Internal, External,
    Controllable or Uncontrollable environment
EPS .... *See* Earnings per share
Equipment 169
Equity 227
Equity capital 200
Estimated data 61
External environment 30

F

Facilities 164
Facility space per employee 164, 231
Fairchild Industries 236
Financial statements
    Interaction with Resources 170
    Role in the flow of the Strategic Plan 31
    Starting point 187
    Three fundamental 169
Financials .... *See* Financial statements
Fixed assets 204
Flow of the Strategic Plan
    Flow chart 29
    Iterative nature 27
Ford Motor Company 76, 82
Forecast data 60

Franklin, Benjamin 1
Functional organization 252
Funds flow statement*See* Sources and uses of funds

G

G&A Expense 232
Gap 237
Gartner Group 72
General and Administrative .... *See* G&A
General Electric
    Aircraft engine business 254
    Innovation of Strategic Planning 5
    Nine-block matrix 123
    Organization 254
    Strategic Business Units 8
    The author and .... 5, i
General Motors 82
General Widgets
    In the 1960's 17
    Market share 95
    Strategies 102, 296
    Strengths and Weaknesses 102, 296
Goals
    Advanced Pumping Systems 152
    Contrasted to Objectives 135
    Defined 135
    International Microwidgets 159, 296
Goethe 133
Gorbachev, Mikhail 41
Gore, Jr., Albert 244
Gross margin 190, 217, 231
Gross profit 194
Guidelines for preparing the plan 23

H

Hardcore Plan 4
Hargrave, Lee i
Hargrave's Law
    Defined 217
    Trend analysis 234
Harvest/divest 126

Head Ski Company
    Mission 33
    Strategy 92
    Strengths and Weaknesses 89, 109
Head, Howard 33
Headcount 162
High-performance computers 58
Historical data
    Need for in the Strategic Plan 25
    Selection of time period 25
Hockey stick
    Creeping 236
    Defined 235
    International Microwidgets 238
Holmes, Sherlock 13
Honeywell 16
Hudson 82
Humphrey, Hubert H. 161
Hurdle rate
    Defined 274
    Establishing 275
Hybrid organization 255

I

IBM 16, 77
Incremental return on investment 225
Indian River Community College i
Industrial Terminal Systems
    Balance sheet 201
    Operating statement 191
    Resources 171
    Revenue projections 188
    Sources and uses of funds 208
Industry attractiveness 125
Inflation
    Consideration of 54
    International Microwidgets 73
Intel 77
Internal environment 30
Internal rate of return 274
International Data Group 72

International Microwidgets
    Balance sheet 211, 300
    Competition 94, 294
    Development of the mission statement 36
    Environment 127
    Evaluation of the Strategic Plan 238
    Fictitious nature 15
    Founding 18
    Goals 159, 296
    Inflation assumption 73
    Introduction to 15
    Market 72
    Market share 94
    Mission 36, 156
    Objectives 155
    Operating efficiency measurements 240
    Operating statement 210, 299
    Opportunities and Threats 130
    Planning horizon 73
    Programs 159
    Resources 178, 296
    Return measurements 238
    Served Market 96
    Sources and uses of funds 214, 300
    Strategic Plan 291
    Strategies 158, 296
    Strengths and Weaknesses 127, 296
Inventories 203
Inventory turns 203, 231
Invest/grow 126
IRR .... *See* Internal rate of return
Issues 22
ITS .... *See* Industrial Terminal Systems

J

Joint venture 265
Just-in-time inventory control 203

K

Kennedy, Florynce R. 244
Kennedy, John F. 106

L

LaSalle 82
Learning curve
    Applicability to International Microwidgets 36
    Boston Consulting Group 116
    Corollary 118
    Defined 117
Leverage 223
Life cycle .... *See* Product life cycle
Line function 257
Lippman, Walter 133
Long-term debt 206

M

Macro planning 246
Mao Zedong 21
Market
    First step after the Mission 42
    High-performance computers 58
    International Microwidgets 72, 293
    Oil-well pumping units 60
    Role in the flow of the Strategic Plan 28
Market cycles 62
Market data
    Constant dollars versus current dollars 54
    Inflation 55
    Preference for current dollars 55
    Primary sources 52
    Quantification 53
    Quantification in dollars 54
    Quantification in units 53
    Secondary sources 52
Market growth
    And market attractiveness 62
    And market share 78
Market measurements 56
Market research 52
Market segmentation
    Defined 47
    International Microwidgets 72
Market share

Chronological data 82
Conflicting data 79
Defined 78
Deutsche Microwidgets 94
Different perspectives 79
General Widgets 95
Importance 78
International Microwidgets 94
Microwidgets Ichiban 94
Oil-well pumping units 84
Restricting analysis to the top competitors .. 82
Market trends 113
Market value 270
Marketing expense 232
Matrix organization 255
Maugham, W. Somerset 76
McKinsey and Company 5, 8
Mensa i
Merger 265
Micro planning 246
Microsoft 77
Microwidgets Ichiban
    Market share 94
    Strategies 99, 295
    Strengths and Weaknesses 98, 295
MIPS 69
Mission
    Advanced Pumping Systems 35
    First step of the Strategic Plan 31
    Head Ski Company 33
    International Microwidgets 36, 292
    Mitsubishi Electric Corporation 34
    Omission of 31
    Role in the flow of the Strategic Plan 28
    Storage Technology Corporation 34
    Three foundational questions 32
Mitsubishi Electric Corporation 34
Multiple linear regression
    Causal variables 66
    Defined 67
    Elasticities 67

Magnetic disk drives 69
R-squared 67
Standard error 67

N

Nash 82
National Security Agency i
NBI 220
NCR 16
Neider, Charles 41
Net operating loss carryforward 199
Net present value
    Defined 271
    Example 275
Nine-block matrix
    Defined 124
    General Electric 123
    Harvest/divest 126
    Industry attractiveness 125
    Invest/grow 126
    SBU business strengths 126
    Selectivity/earnings 126
Nixon, Richard 20
NOL Carryforward .... See Net Operating
    Loss Carryforward

O

Objectives
    Advanced Pumping Systems 142
    Contrasted to Goals 135
    Defined 134
    International Microwidgets 155
    Role in the flow of the Strategic Plan 30
Operating efficiency measurements 230
Operating profit 196
Operating statement
    Defined 169
    Industrial Terminal Systems 193
    Interactions with the balance sheet 192
    International Microwidgets 210, 299
Operational Plan

CASI-RUSCO 248
Defined 22
First year of the Strategic Plan 24
Interfaces with the Strategic Plan 137
Opportunities and Threats
Advanced Pumping Systems 145
International Microwidgets 130
Result of environmental interactions 112
Role in the flow of the Strategic Plan 29
Sources of 106
Optical character recognition 43

Oracle of Delphi 106
Organizational structures 252
Organizations
Business- or product-oriented 254
Functional 252
Hybrid 255
Line functions 257
Matrix 255
Staff functions 257
Storage Technology Corporation 258
Ovid 76

P

P/E .... See Price-to-earnings multiple
People 162
Personnel 163
Planning Horizon
Defined 25
International Microwidgets 73
Selection of 25
With multiple SBU's 25
Plant 164
Plugs on the balance sheet 201
Portes, William
Background 16
With General Widgets 17
Portfolio matrix 120
Cash cows 122
Dogs 122
Question marks 122

    Scaling 123
    Stars 121
Pratt and Whitney 254
Premium 270
Price-to-earnings multiple 222
Principle of Linkages
    Defined 138
    Four steps 139
    Illustrated 141
    Two rules 140
Product life cycle 63
Product-oriented organization 254
Programs
    Advanced Pumping Systems 150
    Defined 135
    International Microwidgets 159
    Role in the flow of the Strategic Plan 30

Q

Question marks 122

R

Reagan, Ronald 41
Receivables financing 205
Resources
    Defined 161
    Equipment 169
    Facilities 164
    Industrial Terminal Systems 171
    Interaction with financial statements 170
    International Microwidgets 178, 296
    People 162
    Role in the flow of the Strategic Plan 30
Retained earnings 206
Return measurements 217
Return on investment 221, 225
Return on sales 200, 218
Revenue projections 188
Revenues per employee 230
Reverse engineering 97
ROI .... *See* Return on investment
Rolls Royce 254

ROS .... *See* Return on sales
R-squared 67
Rule of 70 56
Rusco Electronic Systems 246

S

Sanders Associates i
Sanity checks 216
SBU .... *See* Strategic Business Unit
Secondary valuation techniques 269
Selectivity/earnings 126
Self-Evaluation 29
Served Market
    Defined 44
    Deodorent 48
    Discretion in segmentation 49
    Food processors 47, 50
    International Microwidgets 73, 96
    Magnetic disk drives 68
    Oil-well pumping units 47, 50
    Printers 47, 49
    Spacecraft 47, 50
    Typewriters 44
Shareholders' equity 206
Shutdown 265
Sources and uses of funds
    Defined 169
    Industrial Terminal Systems 208
    International Microwidgets 209, 300
Sources of competitive data
    Competition 86
    Competitive products 85
    Customers 85
    Literature 86
    Third parties 86
Staff function 257
Staffing 251
Standard error 67
Stars 121
Startup 265
Statistical projection techniques 66

Steiner, George 215
Stevenson, Adlai 161
Storage Technology Corporation
    Chapter XI 112
    Corporate Development............................. 268
    Manufacture of magnetic media 14
    Mission 34
    Organization 258
    Strengths and Weaknesses 110
    The author and i
Strategic Business Plan .... *See* Strategic Plan
Strategic Business Unit
    Business strengths 126
    Defined 9
    Identification of 5
Strategic Plan
    Defined 4
    Flow of 27, 185
    Interfaces with the Operational Plan 137
    International Microwidgets 291
    Planning Horizon 25
    Responsibility for 11
    Selection of Planning Horizon 25
    Versus Strategic Business Plan 4
Strategic planner 12
Strategies
    Advanced Pumping Systems 148
    Competitors' 91
    Defined 148
    Deutsche Microwidgets 101, 295
    General Widgets 102, 296
    International Microwidgets 158, 296
    Microwidgets Ichiban 99, 295
    Offensive 114
    Role in the flow of the Strategic Plan 30
    Synthesis of competitors' 91
    Vulnerable 114
Strategy
    Roots of meaning of the word 21
    Versus structure and staffing 251
Strengths .... *See* Strengths and Weaknesses

Strengths and Weaknesses
    Checklist of considerations 88
    Competitors' 87
    Deutsche Microwidgets 100, 295
    General Widgets 102, 296
    Head Ski Company 89, 108
    International Microwidgets 127, 296
    Microwidgets Ichiban 98, 295
    SBU 106
    Storage Technology Corporation 110
Structure 251
Studebaker 82

T

Technology cycles
    Booz Allen and Hamilton 64
    Defined 64
    Examples 64
    Four phases 65
    High-performance computers 58
    Point of sale terminals 44
Thatcher, Margaret 106
The Hargrave Consultancy i
Three S's 250
Top-down planning 246
Total investment 225
Trade payables 205
Trend analysis 234
Trump, Donald 215, 264

U

Ulm, Germany 11
Uncontrollable environment 76
Univac 76
University of Colorado .... 6, 52, ii
University of Maryland i
University of Pennsylvania .... 16, i

V

Validity tests 216
Valuation techniques

Book value 269
Market value 270
Net present value 271
Price-to-earnings 270
Secondary 269

W

Weaknesses .... *See* Strengths and Weaknesses
What-if analysis 191
White, E.B. 183
Widgets
    Defined 16
    Electronic 16
    Microwidgets 18

Z

Zaibatsu 157